Textiles in Daily Life in the Middle Ages

Textiles
in Daily Life
in the Middle Ages

REBECCA MARTIN

The Cleveland Museum of Art

Published in cooperation
with Indiana University Press

A special exhibition at The Cleveland Museum of Art: January 22 through March 17, 1985

Front and back covers: Details of Figure 41, *Border Ornament.*
Frontispiece: Figure 15, *Fragment with the Annunciation to Mary.*

Design by Merald E. Wrolstad
Manuscript editing by Sally W. Goodfellow
Composition by Digital Typographers, Chesterland, Ohio 44026
Printing by Great Lakes Lithograph Company, Cleveland, Ohio 44109

Library of Congress Cataloging in Publication Data
Martin, Rebecca.
  Textiles in daily life in the Middle Ages
  Catalog of an exhibition.
  Bibliography: p.64.
  1. Textile fabrics, Medieval--Exhibitions.
2. Textile fabrics, Medieval, in art--Exhibitions.
3. Art, Medieval--Exhibitions. 4. Cleveland Museum
of Art--Exhibitions. I. Cleveland Museum of Art.
II. Title.
NK8808.M37 1985   746' .094'074017132   84-28492
ISBN 0-910386-80-3

Distributed by Indiana University Press, Bloomington, Indiana 47405

Contents

Acknowledgements

Medieval textiles have held a particular fascination for me since my first trip to Europe in 1971. My interest deepened during 1980-81 when I did research in Europe for my doctoral dissertation on a group of German tapestries. The preparation of this catalogue and the accompanying exhibition has given me opportunity to broaden my interest to include medieval textiles other than tapestries. From the presentation of the initial proposal, James A. Birch, curator of the Department of Art History and Education, has enthusiastically encouraged my efforts. Two directors of the Museum have lent their support: first, Sherman E. Lee (now retired), and then his successor, Evan H. Turner. Special thanks go to Anne E. Wardwell, curator of textiles, for her unflagging enthusiasm and cheerful willingness to offer advice and guidance at every step along the way. Her assistant, Ellen Levine, has graciously assisted with many details, and textile conservator Jane T. Hammond has worked hard and skillfully to prepare the textile objects for exhibition.

My colleagues throughout the Museum have been helpful in many ways. In the Department of Art History and Education I am particularly indebted to assistant curator Katherine Solender, whose careful initial editing of the manuscript led to its significant improvement. Final editing was done by Sally W. Goodfellow, the Museum's associate editor, whose expertise and good humor made the work a pleasure. Chief editor Merald E. Wrolstad is responsible for the beautiful design of the catalogue, while most of the photographs were provided by Museum photographer Nicholas C. Hlobeczy and his assistant Robert Browske, with attention to many details by Nancy Schroeder. Research was expedited by the library staff, particularly Georgina Gy. Toth and Rena Hudgins.

I am grateful to the Philadelphia Museum of Art for the loan of the tapestry *Scene of Courtly Life*. Arrangements for this loan were made by Museum registrar Delbert Gutridge. For the loan of objects from within the Museum I wish to thank textile curator Anne E. Wardwell, curator of early Western art Patrick M. de Winter, curator of paintings Ann T. Lurie, and chief curator of prints and drawings Louise S. Richards and assistant curator Jane Glaubinger. For the handsome installation of the exhibition thanks are due to Joseph Finizia, the Museum's associate designer.

Rebecca Martin
January 1985

Introduction

The Cleveland Museum of Art has an extensive and outstanding collection of textiles with particularly noteworthy holdings from the medieval period, including some acknowledged masterpieces well known to art historians and textile enthusiasts throughout the United States and Europe. Museum visitors may also be familiar with many of them, for they constitute an integral part of the display of paintings, sculptures, and other works of art in the medieval galleries. These permanent galleries have been designed and installed with the goal of demonstrating the dynamic interrelatedness of the various art forms, even while showing each object to its best advantage. The present exhibition, embracing that goal, seeks to focus on a select group of textiles, and to place them within the broader context of medieval art and life.

During the twelfth through the fifteenth centuries, or the High and Late Middle Ages, a largely non-reading European populace was particularly susceptible to the visual language of art. In one sense, art was a tool of the dominant institutions of society—the Catholic church and the aristocracy. They used architecture, sculpture, painting, tapestry, and objects of gold, enamel, and ivory as the backdrop and accoutrements for the pageantry and ceremony whereby they impressed others with their position and power. Sumptuous and costly textiles were an indispensable component of this display. Even the common laborer clad in rough woolens or linens had ample opportunity to admire the precious silks, cloths of gold, and tapestries that either adorned the churches on feast days or draped the streets for princely processions and entertainments.

Perhaps the most familiar and best loved of medieval textiles are the splendid tapestries, which, covering large expanses of museum walls, command recognition by their very size, as well as by richness of color, charm of subject and design, and perfection of craftmanship. A vast wealth of documentation testifies to their importance in the Middle Ages. But in addition to the imposing tapestries that draped the walls of church and palace alike, a variety of textiles brightened the interiors and even the façades of medieval buildings. Precious fabrics, a mark of position and privilege, were acquired at great cost to be used and reused, recorded in inventories, and handed down as valuable inheritance.

Because they were so often functional as well as decorative, many medieval textiles survive only in fragmentary, sometimes heavily worn, condition. Still beautiful despite these losses, they acquire new significance when imagined in their original contexts. The seventeen textile objects in the exhibition—sixteen from the Museum collection and one lent by the Philadelphia Museum of Art— have been selected to represent a variety of medieval luxury fabrics as well as a wide range of uses for them. Because the textiles alone cannot always tell the full story, other objects have been included—sculptures, panel paintings, and manuscript illuminations. They show textiles in use, whether in costumes and church vestments, or in interior furnishings, both secular and ecclesiastical. They also demonstrate the influence of textiles on artists working in other media, from the sculptor who imitated a geometrically patterned silk on the polychromed mantle of a statue to the painter whose composition was inspired by a tapestry.

In the two essays that follow, the textiles and other objects in the exhibition are discussed under the general headings of textiles in ecclesiastical usage and textiles in secular life. By thus considering silks, brocades, velvets, tapestries, and embroideries as part of the "fabric" of medieval life, a key is provided for better understanding an age when both religious ceremony and secular pageantry owed to precious fabrics a large measure of their splendor.

Part One

Textiles in Ecclesiastical Settings

Churches probably provided the most frequent opportunities for laymen to admire the splendors of woven silk from Italy and Spain, tapestries from the North, and embroidery from all corners of Europe. Plush carpets sometimes covered the steps of the high altar, along with the floor in the choir and in front of the bishop's throne. Tapestries and other costly fabrics were hung on the walls of the choir as well as behind the statues of saints throughout the building. They were draped over the pulpit, the organ, the shrines, and the backs of the choir stalls. The high altar, a major focus of textile adornment, was surrounded and covered with precious fabrics. The writings of contemporary theologians explain the symbolic significance that was attributed to these rich hangings, carpets, and draperies. For Rupert of Deutz (died ca. 1129) the fabrics symbolized the glory that would adorn the Church as the unblemished Bride of Christ in His future kingdom. The liturgist Sicardus (died 1215) interpreted them even more specifically as symbols of the virtues that distinguish the Church as Bride of Christ.[1]

The expenditure of church funds for the ornamentation of ecclesiastical buildings with textiles and other costly objects was not without its critics, and conversely, apologists marshalled arguments in defense of such practices. Sicardus pointed out that through visible textile ornaments the faithful are inspired to seek after the invisible treasures of heaven. One of the most eloquent spokesmen on behalf of art in the Church was Abbot Suger of St. Denis (died 1151), who defended the spiritual value of material splendor with the following words:

11

Thus when—out of my delight in the beauty of the house of God—the loveliness of the many-colored gems has called me away from external cares, and worthy meditation has induced me to reflect, transferring that which is material to that which is immaterial, on the diversity of the sacred virtues: then it seems to me that I see myself dwelling, as it were, in some strange region of the universe which neither exists entirely in the slime of the earth nor entirely in the purity of Heaven . . . .[2]

Although he speaks in this passage not of silk and cloths of gold but of gem-studded reliquaries and liturgical objects, Abbot Suger's argument summarizes the position of many medieval churchmen with regard to all costly ornamentation of church buildings.

It is no surprise that the fabrics that formed an integral part of church ornament and liturgical observance in the Middle Ages have become an invaluable source of knowledge of the textiles of that period and their uses. Fabrics employed in the church had an aspect of sacredness in addition to the preciousness of their materials and thus were carefully maintained in sacristies and treasuries. The extant vestments are most likely the finest ones—those that had been reserved for use on feast days and other special occasions—while the more ordinary vestments worn daily by the clergy have, for the most part, not survived.

By the twelfth century the garments of the clergy had acquired a clear, readable symbolism, which afforded easy recognition of an individual's position in the church hierarchy.[3] The particular garments worn at any given time also corresponded to the function being performed. Thus the priest, deacons, and other clergy portrayed in Hans Baldung's *The Mass of St. Gregory* of ca. 1511 (fig. 1) are attired for the celebration of the Eucharist. Baldung, showing his German penchant for realistic detail, has carefully recorded the vestments of the clergy and the fittings of the altar. The subject of the painting is an event in the life of St. Gregory (Pope Gregory I, ca. AD 540-604), identified here by an inscription in his halo. Once while celebrating the Mass he reportedly experienced a vision of Christ, who appeared on the altar displaying His wounds and surrounded by the instruments of the Passion—the objects with which He was tormented in His last days.[4] In Baldung's painting the

Figure 1. Hans Baldung (called Grien), German, 1484/5-1545. *The Mass of St. Gregory.* Oil on panel (linden?), 35-1/8 x 49-3/16 inches, ca. 1511. Gift of the Hanna Fund, CMA 52.112.

Color Plate I.
*Fragment of a Chasuble
with Orphrey Cross*
(detail; fig. 3 and cat. no. 2).

two deacons kneeling with St. Gregory share this vision, for all three look toward it, raising their hands in astonishment. The deacons wear dalmatics, similar in design but made of differently patterned and colored fabrics, probably velvets. The dalmatic, a shin-length tunic with short sleeves and often split on the sides, is the principal vestment of deacons. It is worn over a longer tunic of white linen called an alb. White linen was prescribed for albs as well as for altar cloths because it could be easily washed and kept spotless and pure. White linen also had symbolic associations as the cloth used for both the swaddling clothes and the shroud of Christ.[5]

In the painting St. Gregory also wears an alb, as was common for bishops and priests, and over it a chasuble, the outermost and principal vestment worn by a priest during the Mass. As such, the chasuble was made usually of the finest available fabric and was often heavily adorned. Because the priest stood facing the altar, with his back to the congregation, the back of the chasuble typically received the greater ornamentation. Decorative bands, called orphreys, have been applied to the back of St. Gregory's

Figure 2. *Back of a Chasuble with Orphrey Cross*. Velvet. Italy, early 15th century. Orphrey cross: embroidery, Bohemia, 15th century. CMA 50.85 (cat. no. 1).

chasuble in the shape of a cross and embellished with a crucifix. A bust of God the Father is dimly visible above. The figure of Christ on the cross looks almost sculptural, as if Baldung meant to represent the relief embroidery popular at the time. With this technique a three-dimensional effect was created through the use of padding. While sumptuous, St. Gregory's chasuble could have been worn by any priest and bears no indication of the papal status of its wearer.

Among the other figures around the altar are, at the far left, a cardinal in a red, hooded, fur-lined vestment and next to him, an acolyte in a white surplice. On the right a man in a garment of pink moiré, or watered silk, almost hides from view a knight of the Order of St. John, recognizable as such by the white Maltese cross applied to his black robe. He has been identified as Erhart Künig, who, commissioned the painting.[6] Baldung has carefully rendered the textile furnishings on and around the altar—the curtains suspended from rods on either side, the white linen altar cloth, the altar frontal with decorative border, and the lozenge-patterned green fabric serving as a carpet on which the three men kneel.

The chasuble worn by Baldung's St. Gregory can be compared with the back of an actual chasuble of the fifteenth century (fig. 2). Like the painted chasuble, the real one is made of a decoratively patterned fabric and adorned with cruciform orphreys embroidered with a religious subject. Medieval vest-

ments were typically constructed from a combination of the finest available materials, sometimes from rather disparate sources. In this case an Italian velvet is combined with a Bohemian embroidered orphrey cross. The orphreys, worked in polychome silks and gold thread, show the Madonna and Child, and SS. Catherine, Dorothy, Ursula, and Barbara; each figure stands under an architectural canopy. Whereas Baldung's choice of the crucifix for the orphreys of St. Gregory's chasuble was appropriate both for the cross form of the bands and for the symbolism of the painting, the reason for the choice of this group of female saints is not known.[7] One might surmise, however, that it was because the four virgin martyrs who accompany the Madonna and Child were favorites in the German-speaking lands; they may also have had some special meaning for the church in which the vestment was worn.

A fragment of a fourteenth-century chasuble of Italian silk displays orphreys of a different type, sometimes called Cologne borders after their place of manufacture (fig. 3 and color pl. I). Here the half-silk bands, woven of silk and linen with gold filé, have stylized, non-figural designs. At the top of the vertical band a pelican feeds its young with its own blood, a familiar symbol of the sacrificial bloodshed of Christ. Other motifs on this panel are the name "Maria" (for the Virgin Mary), an eight-petalled rosette, and a flowering tree. The rosette may be another reference to the Virgin, to whom the Biblical

sobriquet Rose of Sharon was applied, and the tree has been identified as the Tree of Life.[8] Another possibility is that it is a rose bush and also refers to the Virgin. The woven orphrey bands are outlined by narrower bands of embroidery in silk and gold filé on blue velvet.

Once again, the chasuble exemplifies the tendency to combine disparate materials in a single vestment. The German woven bands bearing religious emblems have been applied to a garment made of fourteenth-century Italian silk of completely secular design. For this fabric the artist borrowed from several textile traditions, combining a Chinese phoenix with a European dog and pseudo-Arabic letters in a delicate, graceful asymmetrical design. On a ground of tan silk the pattern is defined in membrane gold, a type of thread made by wrapping strips of gilded animal skin or gut around a linen core. This chasuble has suffered more than fragmentation, for the faded tan silk was red when new and the gold thread would have glistened and sparkled. Still, the design has a freshness and charm reflecting the talent of a textile designer to whom a number of silks have been attributed on the basis of certain recurring motifs and a characteristic style.[9]

Sometimes orphreys survive independently of the vestments of which they were once a part, as is the case with a fragment of a fourteenth-century English example (fig. 4). This embroidery of polychrome silks and metallic

Color Plate II. *The Madonna and Child with Saints* (fig. 6 and cat. no. 4).

threads on linen portrays the Tree of
Jesse, a visualization of the genealogi-
cal tree of Christ as recorded in the
Gospel of Matthew, 1:1-16, which was a
favorite subject of medieval English
embroiderers. A particularly fine example survives on an orphrey in the Musée
Historique des Tissus in Lyon (fig. 5).
The "tree," actually a scrolling
grapevine, springs from the body of the
sleeping King Jesse. Enthroned in the
ogival (reversed curve) fields formed by
its intertwined branches are his son
and grandson the great kings David
and Solomon, then the Madonna and
Child, while three-quarter-length
figures of prophets are contained within
curling tendrils to either side. The
Crucifixion group at the pinnacle
reveals the true significance of the Tree
of Jesse, the fulfillment of the prophesy
of Isaiah: "Then a shoot shall grow
from the stock of Jesse, and a branch
shall spring from his roots" (Isaiah
11:1). The grapevine itself symbolizes
the wine of the Eucharist, thus the
sacrificial death of Christ. As a reminder of the central doctrines of the
Christian faith, the Tree of Jesse was
a fitting subject with which to adorn
liturgical vestments.

Figure 3. *Fragment of a Chasuble with Orphrey
Cross.* Lampas weave. Italy, last third of the 14th
century. Orphrey cross: compound twill weave,
Germany, Cologne, 14th century.
CMA 28.653 (cat. no. 2).

Figure 4. *Orphrey Panel with the Tree of Jesse.* Embroidery. England, third quarter of the 14th century. CMA 49.503 (cat. no. 3).

Figure 5. *Orphrey Panel with the Tree of Jesse.* Embroidery, 13-3/16 x 58-1/4 inches. England, first quarter of the 14th century. Lyon, Musée Historique des Tissus, 25434. Photo: Giraudon/Art Resource, New York, NY.

The Cleveland orphrey shows three of the ancestors of Christ—from top to bottom, Achim, Exechias Rex, and Eliud—identified by the inscribed scrolls they hold. A closely related panel in the Brooklyn Museum has four ancestor figures, while a third, in a private collection, has two. At the bottom of each of these panels the vine springs from a ground of tiny flowers, indicating that none of them showed Jesse as the root of the family tree. Probably another vestment in the set to which the three once belonged included Jesse, the kings David and Solomon, and Christ.[10]

English embroidery, or *opus anglicanum*, of which the Cleveland orphrey is a fine example, was highly prized throughout Europe, particularly in the thirteenth and fourteenth centuries, as indicated by inventories and other documents. The records of the popes from this period mention many embroidered vestments from England, either purchased or received as gifts, and in the Vatican inventory of 1295 *opus anglicanum* is mentioned 113 times.[11] The Cleveland orphrey is one of only nine or ten embroideries of the Tree of Jesse that survive from this "great period" of *opus anglicanum*. These few examples, nevertheless, represent a significant portion of the scant hundred or so surviving English embroideries produced before 1400.[12]

The luxurious vestments worn by the clergy officiating in the Mass complemented the rich outfittings of the altar itself. An altar completely if not lavishly appointed with such textile furnishings can be seen in Baldung's *The Mass of St. Gregory* (fig. 1). The high altar is the spiritual focus of a Christian sanctuary, and most medieval churches were designed to make it the spatial and visual focus as well. The main entrance into the church was almost always at the west end, so that the high altar was located at the opposite end of the long central aisle, or nave. Thus the altar was bathed in light from the east windows, providing, as the sun rose each morning, a recurring reminder of the Resurrection of Christ. As both the sacred location of the celebration of the Eucharist and the center of the worshippers' attention, the altar was lavished with the most beautiful and precious of furnishings, often including embroideries, tapestries, silks, and velvets. From early medieval times it was customary to adorn the front of the altar with an antependium, or altar frontal, which might be made of various materials— metal, carved or painted wood, or fabric—the last being the most common

Figure 6. *The Madonna and Child with Saints.* Tapestry. Germany, Nuremburg, ca. 1490. CMA 39.162 (cat. no. 4).

choice. Fabric antependia were most often of decorative silks, but many were also elaborately embroidered or woven in tapestry technique.[13]

A German tapestry of about 1490 showing the Madonna and Child with saints could have served as an altar frontal in a church in Nuremberg, the city in which it is thought to have been woven (fig. 6 and color pl. II). The figures are gathered in a wall garden, which may be a representation of the *hortus conclusus*, or enclosed garden, a symbol of the perpetual virginity of Mary.[14] Both the Christ Child and his Mother hold pieces of fruit from the tree beside them. They are thus shown to be the new Adam and the new Eve, who have redeemed mankind from the curse of original sin incurred by the first pair when they ate the forbidden

fruit in the Garden of Eden.[15] The tapestry designer has dressed the other holy figures in fashionable, elegant gowns made of pomegranate-patterned fabrics and in richly colored mantles with jewelled borders. St. Catherine, with the sword of her martyrdom, and St. Mary Magdalene, with her jar of ointment, wear elaborate turban-like headdresses; all of the saints have jewelled haloes. St. John the Evangelist, barefoot as a sign of humility, gestures toward the chalice of poison that by virtue of his faith he was able to consume without being harmed. The fourth saint is dressed as a pilgrim with

Figure 7. *The Coronation of the Virgin.* Embroidery. Italy, Florence, first half of the 15th century. CMA 53.129 (cat. no. 5).

Figure 9. *Antependium with St. Catherine in the Central Medallion Flanked by Angels and Doves.* Embroidery. Italy, last quarter of the 15th century. Cusona (Siena), Chiesa di S. Biagio. Photo: Archivi Alinari, Florence.

Figure 8. Lorenzo Monaco, Italian, 1370/71-1425. *The Coronation of the Virgin* (detail). Panel, 1414. Galleria degli Uffizi, Florence. Photo: Archivi Alinari, Florence.

pilgrim's hat, staff, and ankle-length leggings under a short tunic. His attributes seem to correspond most closely to those of St. Jodokus, a saint venerated throughout Germany, especially as a patron saint of pilgrims.[16]

Beyond the garden wall unfolds a hilly landscape with buildings resembling some that can still be seen in the countryside around Nuremberg. The attempt to represent an expansive landscape in the distance reflects the increasing influence on tapestry of contemporary painting, with its concern for convincing spatial settings. Yet the figures, lined up in front of the wall, dwarf the distant landscape and are not yet convincingly situated within it.

An embroidered tondo of the Coronation of the Virgin made in Florence in the first half of the fifteenth century once formed the central portion of another fabric antependium (fig. 7 and color pl. III). Inventory records along

with a few surviving examples (fig. 12) indicate that the Coronation of the Virgin was a favorite subject for embroidered antependia in the fourteenth and fifteenth centuries.[17] The scene, also familiar from Gothic sculpture, mosaic, and painting (fig. 8), is not actually described in the Bible. However, Apocryphal sources relate that on the third day after her death Mary ascended bodily into Heaven to sit at the right hand of her Son. Medieval theologians interpreted certain Old Testament passages as prophesies of this miracle and of the ensuing coronation of Mary as Queen of Heaven.[18] The scene in this embroidered tondo depicts the moment when Christ places a silver crown on his Mother's humbly bowed head. Beside Mary is St. Verdiana, patronness of Florence, significant because the altar frontal of which the tondo was part was originally in the Cloister of Santa Verdiana in Florence.

Figure 10. *Scenes from the Life of the Virgin*. Embroidery, 6-1/2 x 47-1/4 inches. Italy, Florence, first third of the 14th century. The Toledo (Ohio) Museum of Art, Gift of Florence Scott Libbey.

Figure 11. *Scenes from the Life of the Virgin*. Embroidery. Italy, Florence, first third of the 14th century. CMA 78.36 (cat. no. 6).

Figure 12. Jacopo Cambi, Italian, Florence. *Antependium with Scenes from the Life of the Virgin in the Superfrontal and the Coronation of the Virgin Flanked by Saints in the Main Portion*. Embroidery, signed and dated 1336. Palazzo Pitti, Florence. Photo: Gabinetto fotografico della Soprintendenza ai Beni Artistici e Storici di Firenze.

Beside Christ is St. Anthony Abbot, venerated as the founder of Christian monasticism. Two angels hold a cloth of honor, with gold palmettes, behind the heavenly consorts, while angels make celestial music on earthly instruments of the fifteenth century. In representing the heavenly court the artist has been inspired by terrestrial ones in which precious fabrics of gold and silk draped the walls, cushioned the benches, and carpeted the floors.

This Coronation tondo is a rare survivor of Florentine embroidery of the fifteenth century, a time when *opus florentinum* was greatly prized in Italy and in northern Europe.[19] The arts of painting and embroidery were closely linked in Florence, where prominent painters sometimes provided designs for embroiderers.[20] The Coronation roundel has been associated with the circle of Lorenzo Monaco, particularly Paolo Schiavo, who early in his career was probably a student of Lorenzo.[21] The figures of Mary and Christ from Lorenzo's famous altarpiece in the Uffizi Gallery demonstrate the dependence of the embroidery's designer on Florentine painting of the same period (fig. 8). For the Coronation roundel the embroiderer used a technique known as *or nué*, or shaded gold, a type of surface couching employed by Florentine needleworkers in their attempts to rival painters in the creation of illusionistic contrasts of light and shade. Gold filé thread laid down in parallel lines from side to side of an area to be embroidered was fastened with a stitch where it turned on reaching the outline. The gold was then shaded with colored silks to create the effect of modeling: in the shaded areas of the design the silk couching stitches were worked so thickly that the gold was almost hidden, while in lighter areas the intervals between stitches were gradually increased until, in the highlights, the gold was exposed in all its brilliance. In some areas, such as the Virgin's mantle, silk alone—worked in split stitch—was used to approximate the delicate shading possible in a painting.

The antependium of which the Coronation tondo was the central part probably resembled the one preserved in the parish church of Cusona, near Siena (fig. 9). In the center is a badly damaged roundel embroidered with the figure of St. Catherine. It is flanked by two angels who gently touch its gold border, while doves and sunrays fill the remainder of the red velvet field. Although only this and one other fabric altar frontal with an embroidered central medallion survive, the type is well evidenced by painted copies on the fronts of a group of altars in the church of Santo Spirito, Florence.[22]

In the fourteenth and fifteenth centuries fabric altar frontals were often enriched by the addition of a narrow overhang of fabric extending the length of the altar frontal along the top edge, such as the one adorning the Cusona antependium (fig. 9). Typically the finest, costliest textiles were employed for these "superfrontals," which might be embroidered in silk and gold, sometimes even with pearls. Because the area to be embroidered was so small, superfrontals did not normally have narrative depictions, but rather simpler motifs such as a row of seated figures or portrait busts.[23] There were exceptions, however, such as an extraordinary fourteenth-century embroidered Florentine superfrontal with scenes from the life of the Virgin (figs. 10, 11). Now shared equally between the art museums of Cleveland and Toledo, the panel has a total of twelve scenes, six on each half. The scenes of the Toledo portion recount the Apocryphal story of the Virgin's birth and early life. The Cleveland portion continues with the Annunciation to Mary, the Adoration of the Shepherds, the Adoration of the Magi, the Presentation of Christ in the Temple, and Christ among the Doctors. The final scene shows the Assumption of the Virgin, which must have been preceded by one or more intermediary scenes, certainly including the Death of the Virgin. With only one additional scene, the entire length of the superfrontal would have measured roughly 104-3/4 inches, an average width for an altar frontal. By contrast, an unusually long antependium—with superfrontal—measuring 167-1/4 inches in length is preserved in the Pitti Palace (fig. 12). It provides some indication of the original appearance and use of the superfrontal now housed in two Ohio museums. Signed by Jacopo Cambi and dated 1336, it shows the Coronation of the Virgin in the center, flanked by angels and saints. The superfrontal,

23

bordered with fringe, has eleven scenes from the Life of the Virgin.

Like the tondo with the Coronation of the Virgin (fig. 7), the Cleveland/Toledo superfrontal shows the definite influence of contemporary Florentine painting. The compositions of the various scenes have been compared to frescoes by Giotto and his followers, although the design of the superfrontal has been attributed nonetheless to a lesser artist who was inspired by Giotto's paintings.[24] The embroidery is somewhat abraded, due in part to its having been used in a place exposed to continual friction from the robes of the priests officiating at the altar. Precious materials were used. The background is couched in gold filé, as are the haloes and certain other details. The remainder of the embroidery is in colored silks, primarily worked in split stitch.

One of the particular treasures of Cleveland's medieval and textile collections is a large German white-on-white embroidery that may have served as a curtain to conceal the altar and the sacraments from the view of the congregation during the period of abstinence and atonement, from the beginning of Lent until the Wednesday of Holy Week (fig. 13).[25] Evidence provided by inventories together with surviving examples shows that the use of such Lenten cloths was widespread in England, France, and Germany from the eleventh century on.[26] On certain occasions during Lent the curtain might be drawn back to reveal the altar, particularly for mass on Sundays in commemoration of the Resurrection of Christ. On the Wednesday before Easter when the words of Luke were read, "And the curtain of the temple was torn in two" (Luke 23:45), the curtain was removed, dramatically restoring the altar to public view.[27]

24

Figure 13. *Lenten Cloth.* Embroidery, 60-3/4 x 147-1/2 inches, ca. 1330-50. Germany, Hesse, Convent of Altenberg an der Lahn. Purchase from the J.H. Wade Fund, CMA 48.352.

Figure 14. Detail of Figure 13. Quatrefoil with St. Elisabeth of Hungary.

The subject of the Cleveland curtain is appropriate for the Lenten season: the large central quatrefoil depicts the Crucifixion, while around it are scenes that relate the story of the Resurrection. Other quatrefoils contain the symbols of the four evangelists and a series of saints. The rest of the ground is filled with fanciful renderings of animals, birds, hybrid creatures, geometric ornament, and tracery. Among the saints represented in the embroidery, one is of particular historical interest: in the quatrefoil just to the left of the Crucifixion St. Elisabeth of Hungary, Countess of Thuringia, is shown feeding a sick person reclining on a bed (fig. 14). St. Elisabeth, venerated for her piety and good works to the poor and sick, had a daughter named Gertrude, whom she placed in the Abbey of Altenberg an der Lahn. Gertrude became abbess there in 1248, remaining so until her death in 1297. The nuns of Altenberg were thus especially devoted to the cult of St. Elisabeth, who had been beatified in 1235. She also appears in an embroidered altar cloth from the same convent, now in New York.[28]

The Cleveland Lenten cloth is one of three or four surviving whitework embroideries from the Premonstratensian convent of Altenberg an der Lahn.[29] This type of embroidery, which employs white linen thread on a white linen ground, was widely practiced by German nuns and was known as *opus teutonicum* in medieval inventories. While the use of these simple, readily available and inexpensive materials

Figure 15. *Fragment with the Annunciation to Mary.* Lampas weave. Italy, last third of the 14th century. CMA 31.61 (cat. no. 7). See also frontispiece

so that they could be cut apart for use as orphreys, a less expensive substitute for embroidered orphreys.[33] Larger pieces might also be used for entire vestments. Judging from inventories and the number of surviving examples, the Annunciation was a popular subject for these figural silks. At least eight museums own pieces of the silk illustrated in figure 15, which is just one of the several known variations on the Annunciation motif.[34]

Woven in lampas weave of blue silk with white silk for the faces and hands and membrane gold for the remainder of the design, the Annunciation is portrayed very simply, without any suggestion of an architectural setting. Both the Archangel Gabriel and Mary kneel in a field of dainty flowers:[35] He bears a staff in one hand and raises the other in salutation, while she crosses her arms devoutly on her breast and inclines her head in humility. Two birds accompany them, the one swooping down from above probably representing the Holy Spirit. A star appears above the wings of the angel.

In addition to the highly visible vestments and altar furnishings of precious fabrics, medieval churches also housed smaller textile objects, such as reliquary wrappings, which were seldom, if ever seen. The fervent veneration in

was probably due in part to the relative poverty of the convents, white linen was also the preferred material for certain liturgical textiles, particularly for those to be used during Lent. Only eight different types of stitches were used to create the design of the Cleveland cloth as compared to a greater variety of stitches used on the altar cloth from Altenberg in the Metropolitan Museum, New York. The facial features of the Cleveland hanging are not indicated, whereas those of the New York cloth are. The relative simplicity of the larger Cleveland panel may relate to its original function. If indeed it was used to conceal the altar during Lent, then the light of the east windows would have shown through it so that the figures were silhouetted against the light. For this effect the

variety and detail of the stitches would have mattered less than their density.[30] Although the faces are now blank, it is possible that they were once delineated with colored thread, perhaps of silk, which has worn away. Some existing whitework embroideries do have traces of colored threads used either in this way or to accentuate the outlines of the figures.[31]

While many altar frontals and other church hangings were of tapestry-woven or embroidered fabrics, others were made of patterned silks. Inventory descriptions of silks with religious figural subjects, an innovation of Italian silk weaving in the second half of the fourteenth century, indicate that they were used for vestments and altar hangings.[31] Such fabrics were often woven in horizontal or vertical bands

26

Figure 16. *Fragment of a Woven Bag.* Tapestry. France, second half of the 13th century. CMA 39.37 (cat. no. 8).

each with four pointed shields with armorial bearings. Against what was originally a white ground the shields are woven of polychrome silks and gold filé. In the interstices between them is either a rosette or a very abstract floral motif. The four coats of arms repeated on the tapestry are: above, alternately De Châtillon, count of Blois, and the six fleurs-de-lis of France; below, alternately Flanders and De Dreux, duke of Brittany. At the time when the tapestry was made, probably in the second half of the thirteenth century, Blois, Flanders, and Brittany were fiefs of France. The technique of weaving small-scale tapestries of silk and metallic thread originated with Muslim weavers in Spain and must have been brought by them to northern Europe. Financial records and inventories indicate that "Saracenic" (Muslim) weavers were living and working in and around Paris and in Flanders in the thirteenth century.[41]

A better-preserved example of the typical medieval reliquary bag is constructed of silk patterned with tan fleurs-de-lis on a blue ground (fig. 17). The silk fabric of compound twill weave might be Spanish or Italian. Compound

the Middle Ages of relics of saints had given rise to an avid enthusiasm among churchmen and laymen alike for acquiring them; therefore, for the protection and display of relics special containers, or reliquaries, of myriad description were fashioned. They ranged from bags of tapestry or silk to ornate gold vessels with crystal "windows" for viewing the sacred contents. Inside reliquaries of metal, enamel, or ivory the relics were often wrapped in small pieces of silk.[36]

With remarkable frequency, fabric bags known as *aumônières* made their way into churches to serve as reliquaries, which accounts for the large number of these once-fashionable ac-

cessories.[37] The *aumônière*, or alms bag, was usually a trapezoid-shaped bag with rounded upper corners and a flap closure. Such bags originated as containers for alms to be distributed to the poor, but later were used to carry any personal items such as keys or jewelry. They were worn suspended from the belt.[39] A battered, discolored piece of silk and gold tapestry is a fragment from a bag that evidently functioned as a container for relics in the church in Cologne where it is said to have been found (fig. 16). A larger fragment of the same bag is preserved in the Schnütgen Museum in that city.[40] This fragment has a design of two horizontal rows, twill weave was commonly used for Spanish silks of the thirteenth century, whereas lampas weave became the preferred technique in the fourteenth. Italian silk weaving of the thirteenth century was closely related to that of Spain, so that it is often difficult to assign a fabric to one country or the other, a situation that changed in the fourteenth century when Italian silks became quite distinctive. The fleur-de-lis pattern was as widely used in Spain and Italy as in France, where fleurs-de-lis had been adopted as the arms of the royal house, probably during the reign of Louis VII (1120-80).[42] This reliquary bag, formerly preserved in a church in Saint-Omer (Pas-de-Calais), France, may have been made of silk from a worn-out vestment. Because of their great value, silks from old vestments were commonly salvaged to be reused for reliquary bags and other small objects.[43]

While many medieval tapestries with religious subjects were intended for use in churches, others were used as private devotional objects. A small Flemish tapestry, roughly twenty-eight inches square, with the symbolic subject of the Mystical Grapes, was probably used in this way (fig. 18). In a circular field enclosed within a square the Holy Family is seen in half-length, a compositional format often employed for devotional images.[44] Mary and Joseph concentrate their attention on the Christ Child, who stares out at the viewer as he squeezes juice from a bunch of grapes into a chalice. The subject, also

Figure 17. *Reliquary Bag*. Compound twill weave. Spain, Mudejar(?), 13th century. CMA 74.101 (cat. no. 9).

known from three other extant tapestries, was inspired by a passage from the Apocryphal Book of Ecclesiasticus: "He reached his hand into the cup and poured forth the blood of the grape".[45] The image symbolizes the sacrament of the Eucharist, or the shedding of Christ's blood for the remission of sin. Other less immediately apparent symbols can be seen: for example, the crossed orb on which the Child rests his left hand signifies the universality of the salvation he offers, while the marked books placed so as to form a

cross probably refer to the Old Testament and its prophesies. Perhaps the same interpretation applies to the open book that three angels are reading, but it might, in fact, represent the New Testament fulfillment of those prophesies.[46]

The Eucharistic theme of the tapestry may have been inspired by the Cult of the Holy Blood, one of the manifestations of late medieval piety and mysti-

Color Plate III.
*The Coronation
of the Virgin*
(detail of lute-playing angel;
fig. 7 and cat. no. 5).

Figure 18. *The Mystical Grapes.* Tapestry. Flanders, ca. 1500. CMA 73.77 (cat. no. 10).

Figure 19. Follower of Hans Memling, Netherlandish, ca. 1440-1494. *Madonna and Child.* Panel, ca. 1485-90. CMA 34.29 (cat. no. 18).

cism. Meditating on the blood shed by Christ was one way for the faithful to share in his agony and to realize fully the meaning of his sacrificial death. The Crusaders had brought back to Europe vials of what they believed to be Christ's blood, thereby fostering the growth of the cult. The production of this and other Flemish tapestries with the same theme may be connected to the existence of a relic of the Holy Blood

in the Flemish city of Bruges, where since the early fourteenth centuy it had been carried each year in a procession around the city.[47]

The tapestry is woven of wool, silk, and metallic threads on a wool warp. The silver areas in the Virgin's mantle and in the cloths of honor hanging behind the Child and behind the three angels consist of flat strips of silver twisted around a yellow silk core. The original gilding has almost completely worn away. Although the wool threads have faded, the attempt to rival painting in the subtlety of shading and modelling in the faces and hands is still apparent. The designer's debt to late fifteenth-century Flemish painting can be demonstrated by comparing the tapestry to a small half-length composition of the Virgin and Child by a follower of Hans Memling (fig. 19). Both portrayals of the Virgin employ the same facial type—an oval face with small chin, small mouth with full lower lip, long nose slightly protruding at the tip, heavily lidded downcast eyes, delicate brows, and a high forehead. Also very similar are Mary's hairstyle and the drapery folds of her full oversleeves, as well as the elongated head and the facial features of the Child.

Figure 20. Attributed to Stephan Lochner, German, died 1451. *The Virgin Mary Crowned by Angels.* Panel, ca. 1441. CMA 68.20 (cat. no. 19).

Color Plate IV.
Accidia and Her Court
(fig. 27 and cat. no. 20).

The cloth of honor so frequently featured in late Gothic art is simply a curtain of precious fabric suspended behind a saint as a sign of veneration. The motif must reflect the way luxurious fabrics were used in courtly settings to drape thrones and to form baldachins over the heads of the powerful so that they were constantly seen against a backdrop of lavish textiles. Another devotional image, a small panel of *The Madonna and Child Crowned by Angels*, attributed to the young Stephan Lochner, celebrates the Virgin as Queen of Heaven (fig. 20). Mary's slight, doll-like figure, made substantial by the bunched folds of a brilliant red mantle over a fur-trimmed gown of the same color, is set off against a gold-brocaded green and black cloth of honor.[48]

The artist has rendered the curtain with a keen eye for detail. It is suspended from a rod by delicate red threads attached to brass rings. The top edge is trimmed with blue, gold, and red braid; the bottom, with a blue and white silk fringe. The curtain itself is made of an Italian pomegranate fabric. In the first half of the fifteenth century Italian silk design gradually came to be almost completely dominated by the pomegranate motif, which appeared in countless variations throughout the century. Deriving from Far and Near Eastern lotus blossom and palmette designs, the so-called pomegranate is sometimes exactly that, but may also be a pine cone, an artichoke, or a fanciful fruit bearing little

Figure 21. Master E.S., German, active ca. 1440-68. *The Madonna Enthroned with Eight Angels.* Engraving, dated 1467. CMA 48.170 (cat. no. 23).

resemblance to any of these. The cone or fruit is centered in a large-lobed leaf form, often of ogival configuration.[49]

Stephan Lochner has been credited with introducing pomegranate fabrics into the Cologne School of painting, where by mid-century they had become the most frequently represented type of textile.[50] The use of carefully observed

and rendered Italian silks in fifteenth-century Northern panel paintings is a phenomenon to which scholars have devoted some attention, with fruitful results for historians of textiles and paintings alike.[51] At a time when Italian silks were flooding Northern markets through the agency of the Hanseatic League and of Italian merchants in Bruges, Paris, and London, painters seem to have had ready access to these luxury goods. The recurrence of some of the same textiles in paintings by Lochner and his followers has been interpreted as evidence that his workshop owned either pieces of certain fabrics or patterns that could be used in representing them.[52]

An engraving by the Master E. S. demonstrates a different but related use by a German artist of an Italian pomegranate fabric in an image of the Madonna and Child (fig. 21). The textile, strikingly similar to the one in the Lochner panel, drapes the back of the Virgin's imposing architectural throne. The pattern is partially obscured by the Dove of the Holy Spirit, a crown designating the Virgin as Queen of Heaven, and the letter "M" for Mary. The fabric canopy sheltering the throne is almost plain, adorned only with a simple border trim and few stripes. But the engraver's "urge to ornamentalize" takes over again in the patterning of

Figure 22. *Mantle for a Statue of the Virgin.* Lampas weave. Spain, Hispano-Islamic, 15th century. CMA 29.975 (cat. no. 11).

Mary's gown, the pillow cushion, and the dalmatic worn by the angel kneeling to the left of the throne.[53]

Just as painters and engravers would include sumptuous costumes and hangings based on real textiles in their paintings and prints, so too did medieval sculptors often enhance the beauty and realism of their statues with polychromy in imitation of the precious textiles found in contemporary costumes. In addition to such painted ornament, statues of the Virgin were sometimes draped with real silk mantles such as the one in the Cleveland Museum made of fifteenth-century Hispano-Islamic silk (fig. 22). Tradition holds that it was part of the booty captured at the conquest of Granada in 1491-92, after which it found its way into a church, probably as a votive offering from one of the victors.[54] The small size would indicate that it was used to adorn a statue.[55] Pieced together from several pieces of silk, the mantle has been padded with cotton and quilted. It is lined with a thin red taffeta. The striped silk in lampas weave is of a type for which Granada was famous during the Nasrid dynasty up until the eve of the conquest. The design includes escutcheons evidently based on that of the Nasrid rulers. The Naskhi inscriptions translate "Glory to our Lord, the Sultan." The use of such an Islamic textile in a Christian church was not uncommon in Spain.[56]

The use of precious fabrics of silk and gold for the burial clothes, shrouds, and grave furnishings of important and

wealthy individuals in the Middle Ages is well attested to not only by tombs that have been opened but also by the literature and documents of the period.[57] The preservation of several fragments of a beautiful thirteenth-century Hispano-Islamic silk and gold tapestry results from their reuse as ornaments on the grave clothes of the bishop of Barcelona, Don Arnaldo de Gurb (died 1284). One of the largest and best-preserved fragments, now in the Cleveland Museum, has two medallions inwoven in tapestry technique into a tabby ground (fig. 23). In one, two turbaned men face each other on either side of a stylized tree. They hold up small flasks as if about to drink. In the other, a turbaned horseman seems to approach the men in the first medallion, pointing toward them with his raised hand. The roundels portray two ancient, recurrent themes of Islamic art, the Banquet and the Hunt. Both are symbols of Paradise. The Kufic inscriptions ornamenting the frames of the medallions proclaim "There is no god but Allah."

Originally these sadly faded, discolored medallions formed part of a luxurious textile, probably a wall hanging, which has been photographically reconstructed on the basis of a comparable textile that survives intact (fig. 24).[58] Apparently the textile had seen many years of use before it was appropriated for the burial of Bishop Gurb. Although its exact use in the tomb is not known—whether as garment, furnishing, or shroud—it was almost certainly not

35

Figure 23. *Roundels with Scenes of the Celestial Banquest and Hunt.* Tapestry inwoven in tabby ground. Spain, Hispano-Islamic, probably Almería, first half of the 13th century. From the tomb of Don Arnaldo de Gurb, Bishop of Barcelona (died 1284). CMA 66.368 (cat. no. 12).

Figure 25. The coffin of Jimenez de Rada, Archbishop of Toledo (died 1247), when it was opened in 1908, showing the rich set of ecclestiastical vestments. Photo: Moreno.

Figure 24. Hypothetical reconstruction of the original form of the Bishop Gurb textile (Figure 23); the overall measurements would have been approximately 29 x 43 inches.

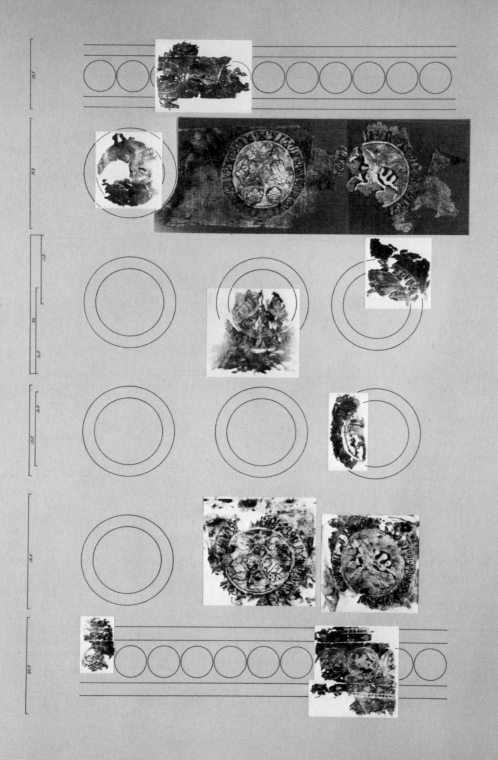

used in its original form. Very likely the hanging was cut apart to be used as ornamental bands, or galloons, on the bishop's garment. The vestments in which the Archbishop of Toledo was buried in 1247 were adorned in this way with orphrey panels made from Hispano-Islamic silks inscribed with Arabic benedictory phrases (fig. 25).

1. Braun 1924b, p.225. On Rupert of Deutz and Sicardus see Cross 1958, pp. 1188, 1253. On the symbolism of the Church as Bride of Christ see Katzenellenbogen 1984, pp. 59-65.

2. Panofsky 1964, pp. 63-65.

3. On the history and significance of ecclesiastical vestments see Hayward 1971; Schimansky 1971; Chicago 1975, pp. 25-52; Mayer-Thurman 1975.

4. On the iconography of the Mass of St. Gregory see Schiller 1968, 2: 240-42, and Cologne 1982.

5. Mayer-Thurman 1975, p. 15.

6. Cleveland 1974, p. 161.

7. The cruciform orphrey adorned with a crucifix was a popular type in sixteenth-century Germany and was frequently used in portrayals of the Mass of St. Gregory. See, for example, Cologne 1982, figs. 15, 19, 21, 22, 24.

8. Scheyer 1932, pp. 57-58.

9. The Cleveland Museum of Art owns another piece of silk that has been attributed to the same designer. See Wardwell 1984, cat. no. 19. For a discussion of the artist's style and further bibliography see Wardwell 1976/77, pp. 200-202.

10. Riefstahl 1950, pp. 5-13, with illus.

11. Christie 1938, pp. 2-3.

12. For discussion of the other Tree of Jesse embroideries see Christie 1914, and Christie 1938, pp. 112-23.

13. Braun 1924a, 2: 1-132; Braun 1937, cols. 441-59.

14. The closed garden of the Song of Songs (4:12) was interpreted by medieval theologians as a prophetic reference to Mary's virginity; see Freeman 1976, p. 136.

15. Metford 1983, p. 33. For an in-depth study of Mary as the New Eve see Guldan 1966, pp. 117-58.

16. This figure has been identified variously as St. Henry, St. Sebald, and St. Jodokus, all of whom were pilgrims of noble lineage. Kurth 1926, 1: 273, identified him as St. Henry (Heinrich), by which she must have meant St. Henry of Ebrantshausen. Luitpold (Herzog in Bayern) 1926, 1: 79, recognized him as St. Sebald. St. Sebald did have special meaning for Nuremberg, the likely place of the tapestry's manufacture. His cult was centered in that city, where his remains are housed in the church bearing his name. Against the identification of the pilgrim saint in the tapestry as St. Sebald, two facts should be considered. This saint is almost always shown holding a small model of his church, which is missing here. Moreover, the tapestry is reported to have come not from the Church of St. Sebald but from the Church of St. Lawrence, where the saint would have been less important. On the attributes of SS. Henry, Jodokus, and Sebald see Braun 1943, cols. 319, 363-65, and 640-42, respectively.

17. Gravenkamp 167, 1: 273-74. King 1965, pp. 15-25, discusses a fourteenth-century Venetian antependium with the Coronation and other related examples. Nine Florentine embroideries of the Coronation were listed in the inventory of the Duke of Berry for 1403/05. See Grönwoldt 1961, pp. 55-57.

18. Mâle 1972, pp. 253-58; Katzenellenbogen 1964, pp. 56-59.

19. Grönwoldt 1961, p. 33.

20. Kurth 1931, p. 455; Cavallo 1960. A fourteenth-century artist's handbook by Cennino Cennini (1960 ed., pp. 105-6) includes specific instructions for painters who must supply designs to embroiderers.

21. Longhi 1940, p. 188; Degenhart and Schmitt 1968, 1/2: 421-22; Fremantle 1975, p. 523.

22. Markowsky 1973, pp. 105-40.

23. Braun 1924a, 2: 75-84; Braun 1937, cols. 448-50.

24. Grönwoldt 1969, p. 352; Wardwell 1979, pp. 326-27.

25. This suggstion was offered by Shepherd (1953). Engelmeier 1961, pp. 12-13, has argued that the Cleveland embroidery was intended as an altar cloth to be laid upon the altar so that the whimsical figures under arcades at either side would hang just over the edges.

26. Braun 1924a, 2: 148-51, cites numerous inventories and documents. See also Kroos 1970, p. 163.

27. Braun 1924a, 2: 151-54.

28. Illustrated in Rorimer 1930, pl. opp. p. 10; or see Schuette and Müller-Christensen 1964, figs. 160-64, esp. fig. 162.

29. See Rorimer 1930, pp. 10-13; Von Wilckens 1960, pp. 5- 20; Wagner 1963, pp. 22-27.

30. Shepherd 1953, pp. 10, 15.

31. Aldenkirchen 1885, pp. 264-65; Müller 1944, p. 103; Wagner 1963, pp. 3, 12, 27; Von Wilckens 1975, p. 124.

32. Grönwoldt 1968, p. 82; Wardwell 1976/77, pp. 189-91.

33. Underhill 1931, p. 65; Detroit 1959, p. 75.

34. Grönwoldt 1968, p. 84, cites an inventory of Notre Dame, Paris, from 1416 that records a gift to the cathedral of two Annunciation textiles in 1385 by Queen Isabelle of Bavaria. Other pieces of the same textile owned by The Cleveland Museum of Art are preserved in the following collections: Nuremberg, Germanisches Nationalmuseum; Vienna, Österreichisches Museum für angewandte Kunst; Berlin, Kunstgewerbemuseum; Brussels, Musée Cinquantenaire; London, Victoria and Albert Museum; Florence, Museo Nazionale; Boston, Museum of Fine Arts.

35. The iconography with both the Virgin and Gabriel kneeling was probably derived from a description of the Annunciation in the Pseudo-Bonaventura's *Meditationes vitae Christi*, cap. iii (Robb 1936, p. 485).

36. Such is the case, for example, with the Gertrudis Portable Altar in The Cleveland Museum of Art. This altar and reliquary contains small bones of several saints, wrapped in pieces of silk (Von Falke 1930, p. 106). These silk wrappings are visible in the photograph reproduced in de Winter 1985, fig. 39.

37. Wentzel 1937, 1: 397.

38. Ibid., p. 393.

39. See Gay 1887, 1: 776; Witte 1926, pl. 46, no. 2, and p. 18; Wentzel 1937, 1: 393; Von Wilckens 1981, pp. 280-82.

40. Cologne 1926, pl. 46, no. 2, and p. 18.

41. Dehaisnes 1886, 1: 63, 194, 237, 256.

42. Uden 1968, p. 91.

43. An interesting example of the reuse of silk is the skirt said to have been worn by the mother of St. Elisabeth of Hungary at her coronation. Later the skirt was given to a church, where it was used to make a chasuble. When the chasuble was worn out, it was cut into small pieces and used to wrap relics. See Munich 1955, cat. no. 30.

44. On the use of the half-length composition for devotional paintings see Ringbom 1965, pp. 39ff.

45. Ecclesiasticus 50:16 (in the English translation from the Greek, this passage is found in 50:15). The other Flemish tapestries with the same theme are illustrated by Wardwell 1975, pp. 17-23.

46. For a thorough discussion of the iconography see Wardwell 1975.

47. Ibid., p. 22.

48. Stechow 1969, p. 309, attributes Lochner's treatment of the scarlet robes and his use of the brocaded curtain to the influence of Netherlandish painting, especially that of Bruges, and particularly the work of Jan van Eyck.

49. On the development of the pomegranate design in Italian silk weaving see Cole 1899, pp. 70-95, and Markowsky 1976, pp. 51-54.

50. Klesse 1960, p. 221.

51. Wardwell 1976/77, pp. 177-78, provides a state-of-the-research summary of such studies, to which her own article becomes a substantial contribution.

52. Klesse 1960, pp. 220ff.

53. Philadelphia 1967, unpaginated [p. 13].

54. Underhill 1930, p. 73.

55. For example, a fourteenth-century statue of the Madonna and Child in the Staatliches Museum in Schwerin is still outfitted with a mantle pieced together from fourteenth-and fifteenth-century Italian silks as well as a dress and mantle for the Child. See Schwerin 1983, cat. no. 10, pp. 8 (illus.), 12.

56. Underhill 1930, p. 73.

57. See Michel 1852, 1: 115-58, on the various uses of precious fabrics in the burial customs of the Middle Ages. For a descriptive account by the twelfth-century monk Reginald of Durham of the burial clothing and grave wrappings of St. Cuthbert, see Schapiro 1977, pp. 11-12.

58. The textile that inspired the reconstruction is a silk and gold tapestry-weave cushion cover from the tomb of Queen Berenguela of Castile (died 1246) at Las Huelgas de Burgos. See Shepherd 1978, fig. 12, p. 120.

Figure 26. *Curtain.* Lampas weave, 107 x 172-1/2 inches. Spain, Granada(?), 15th century. Purchase, Leonard C. Hanna, Jr., Bequest, CMA 82.16.

Figure 27. *Accidia and Her Court.* Manuscript illumination. Italy, Genoa or Naples (?), late 14th century. CMA 53.152 (cat. no. 20).

Part Two

Textiles in the Secular Realm

Medieval residences—castles and town-houses alike—were sparsely furnished with only a few pieces of heavy, functional furniture to meet basic requirements for seating, eating, sleeping, and storage. For those who could afford them textiles added color, warmth, texture, and a feeling of luxury to otherwise austere interiors.[1] Extensive evidence bears witness to the widespread use of luxury textiles in domestic settings. The most significant testimony is that of surviving examples—wall hangings of many kinds, including monumental tapestries and embroidered hangings, as well as pillow covers, hand towels, tablecloths, and quilts. The manner in which these and other textiles were actually used is illustrated in innumerable panel and manuscript paintings showing scenes of richly appointed secular interiors. Documentation also survives in the form of inventories, which often specify the functions of the various textiles listed. Other records, such as those of merchants and guilds, provide additional information. Finally, medieval literature abounds in references to precious fabrics, reflecting their importance in the daily life of the ruling class.

In European castles and palaces large silk curtains, like the more familiar tapestries, were used to drape the walls; few examples have survived, however. Only three relatively complete silk curtains are presently known: one in the Metropolitan Museum of Art in New York, one in the Cooper-Hewitt Museum also in New York, and one in the Cleveland Museum of Art (fig. 26). Very similar in technique, design, and color, the three curtains are all from Spain and date from the fifteenth century.[2]

The Cleveland curtain is the largest of the three, with two wide side panels joined down the middle by a narrower strip. Woven entirely of silk on a draw-loom, the lampas weave fabric features the characteristic colors of Spanish silks of the so-called Alhambra style: bright red, intense yellow, navy blue, forest green, and white. The decorative elements of the curtain also belong to the repertory of Alhambra-style silks: arches intertwined with braided strap-work, floral arabesques, star patterns, and Arabic inscriptions. However, the way in which the various decorative elements are combined distinguishes the curtain, along with its counterparts in New York, from other silks of this stylistic group. Instead of the stripes that usually fill Alhambra-style silks, all three curtains feature isolated orna-mental areas arranged against a red ground and framed by inscribed borders at top and bottom. In this respect they seem to have been modelled on monu-mental tapestries of the type to which the tapestry roundels from Bishop Gurb's tomb once belonged (see figs. 23, 24).

Within a cartouche inside each arch in the upper border of the Cleveland silk is an inscription in Naskhi script, "There is no conqueror but God"—the motto of the Nasrid dynasty, which ruled Muslim Spain, with Granada as its capital, from 1231 to 1492.[3] The Cleveland curtain was probably woven in Granada during the last century of Nasrid rule. There is some evidence for the use of such curtains in the

Alhambra Palace in that city. In the Hall of Two Sisters nails were discovered high on one wall with threads of silk still hanging from them. Apparently a silk curtain was torn from the nails when the palace was despoiled by the invading Christian armies in the Re-conquest of 1492. The use of large wall hangings is also indicated by the fact that in the private quarters of the Alhambra, stucco embellishment is restricted to the areas around doors and windows. Since Muslim art has virtually no unadorned surfaces, the blank expanses of wall must have been adorned with textiles.[4] Certainly the surviving silk curtains adorned the most sumptuous of Nasrid residences.

An example of a room with silk hang-ings appears in a miniature from a late-fourteenth-century Italian manu-script (fig. 27 and color pl. IV). Here a bedchamber lavishly appointed with silks is the setting for a gathering of the allegorical figure of the vice Accidia (melancholy or boredom) with the ladies of her court. The walls seem to be hung with a colorful, richly brocaded striped fabric of the same type used for the gowns of the two women seated in the foreground. The women casting dice at an octagonal gaming table are seated on cushions, two of which have a design of gold dots, and two others, a knot pattern bordered with bands of vine-scroll ornament. The cushions rest upon a carpet with blue vines on an orange background. The bed cover is of bright red material; tiny white lap dogs with belled collars scamper across it. The

fabrics in the painting are quite unlike Italian silk designs of the time. They were probably inspired by Muslim silks, since the striped fabrics and the pillows with knot motifs recall Hispano-Islamic examples. These colorful and luxurious textiles give the scene the feeling of an opulent Oriental court.

Among the many uses for luxury fabrics, the draping of thrones and the formation of canopies above them were found only in the most aristocratic households. In a French miniature of the last third of the fifteenth century a queen in an ermine-trimmed gown is seated upon a throne equipped with silk coverings and a canopy suspended by ropes from the ceiling (fig. 28). The queen is Medusa, of the Greek legend; she is shown as a beautiful maiden before her transformation into the terrible monster eventually slain by Perseus.[5] The silks used to adorn Medusa's throne resemble the ubiquit-ous fifteenth century pomegranate fab-rics, but the artist took considerable liberty in rendering the design, for it does not exhibit the usual regularity of uniformly repeating pomegranate motifs as seen on comparable fabrics of the period (see fig. 20). A similar fabric has been used to enclose the open ter-race. Another panel behind three ladies in hennin headdresses is suspended before a window and serves to enclose the area around Medusa's throne. The use of textile hangings to shape interior spaces in this way is well known from fifteenth-century panel paintings and manuscript illuminations such as this

one.[6] Other uses of fabrics are illustrated here as well: plain pieces of cloth cover the tops of a cabinet and a chest, and a battle scene in the distance shows the use of fine fabrics for military banners and for horses' caparisons.[7]

Another painting in The Cleveland Museum of Art, a panel from around 1400 with *The Death of the Virgin* by the Master of Heiligenkreuz, shows the use of a luxury fabric as a bedcover or blanket (fig. 29). Although the number of extant textiles that can be identified as bedcovers is very small, bedcovers and hangings made of precious silks are common in miniature paintings of the Gothic period. Further evidence of their usage is found in inventories; for example, an inventory of Thomas, duke of Gloucester, who died in 1397, lists sixteen "beds" of silk and gold, most of them embroidered.[8] The will of Agnès de Faucigny, dated 1262, specifies that her feather bed together with the bedcovers be given to the convent where she was raised.[9] The practice of willing one's bed and its textile furnishings to a hospital or convent indicates the value attached to these objects.[10] Medieval poets sometimes described the luxurious beds of their heroes in great detail, as for example, in Wolfram von Eschenbach's *Parzival* (ca. 1200 - ca. 1210), where Gawain's bed is

Figure 28. Close to Maître François, French, second half of the 15th century. *Queen Medusa Enthroned.* Manuscript illumination, ca. 1470. CMA 24.1015 (cat. no. 21).

43

described as having, among other fine furnishings, a coverlet of green silk and a canopy lined with palmette-patterned silk.[11]

In the Master of Heiligenkreuz's painting the twelve apostles surround the deathbed of the Virgin. In the center St. Peter, the first pope, is shown wearing the papal tiara and a white cope with pearl-incrusted hood. He administers the sacrament of extreme unction while Christ descends from heaven to receive the soul of Mary, represented as a tiny crowned figure clad in white. The Virgin's body, resting upon white sheets, and propped against a gold-colored pillow with tasseled corners, is partially covered by a brocaded fabric featuring a green and gold foliate design on a red ground. Clearly the artist intended to portray a very precious silk and gold cloth, a form of tribute to the spiritual queenship of the Virgin, and thus completely disregarded the truly humble circumstances of the Biblical Mary's life. Pillows on the low bench on which two apostles sit reflect a medieval custom, by which hard, unupholstered benches and chairs were made more comfortable by the use of overstuffed pillows.

In another scene from the Life of the Virgin, the *Annunciation* by the Spanish artist Jaime Ferrer II, Mary

Figure 29. Master of Heiligenkreuz, Austrian, active ca. 1395-1420. *The Death of the Virgin.* Panel, 21 x 26 inches (painted surface), ca. 1400. Gift of Friends of the Museum in Memory of John Long Severance, CMA 36.496.

wears a mantle of dark blue emblazoned with crowned M's—a reference to her eventual coronation as Queen of Heaven (fig. 30). Judging from their frequent representation in works of art, fabrics adorned with initials or monograms were widely used for garments in the late Gothic period.[12] Mary has been interrupted in her study of the Scriptures by the sudden arrival of the Archangel Gabriel, whose words of greeting are inscribed on the scroll unfurling from his left hand. God peers in through a small round window at the left, through which the Dove of the Holy Spirit has entered and now approaches Mary. Three small angels sing praises in a sky filled with lavish molded and gilded leaf ornament. The simplicity of the small structure behind Mary contrasts with the splendor of the gold background and the richly clothed figures, while the still-life elements within the structure add a homely domestic touch to the scene. At the same time, however, they are all familiar religious symbols. Along with the rosary beads, a round wooden pyx (a box to contain the sacred Host), open and closed books signifying Old Testament prophesies and their New Testament fulfillments, and other symbols, is what appears to be a glass water carafe. A water vessel of some type was frequently represented in late medieval depictions of the Annunciation to symbolize Mary's purity.[13] Almost as common was the realistic detail of a hand towel hanging somewhere near the water vessel. In this case, a white linen

or cotton towel with dark blue trim and long fringe is draped over a wooden towel bar. Close inspection reveals the care with which Ferrer has rendered its white-on-white diaper pattern, a design characteristic of damask woven for table linens in the Middle Ages.[14]

Towels of a more elaborate type popular in the late Middle Ages and for several centuries beyond are generally referred to as Perugia towels after the Italian city that was apparently a major center for their production. Perugia towels are of white linen or cotton with patterned horizontal stripes woven of blue-dyed cotton thread. Because the same techniques and kinds of designs were used for centuries in weaving them, these towels are often difficult to date.[15] A towel in the collection of The Cleveland Museum of Art probably dates to around 1500 (fig.31). Woven of cotton, it is decorated with four horizontal blue bands of varying widths. Two of the bands contain repeating motifs of castles, addorsed dogs, and pairs of facing birds, while the widest horizontal stripe has pairs of facing lions separated by trees. A fourth band contains inscriptions separated by rosettes. The single word repeated numerous times in this and in two of the other bands is "amore," meaning love. Some of the inscriptions, as is characteristic for towels of this type, are in mirror reverse, while others are upside down, so that the word "amore" is not always easily legible and becomes simply part of the decoration of repeating motifs. The areas of plain cotton are subtly

adorned with a self-patterned weave of chevrons or, over most of the towel, a diaper pattern closely resembling that of the towel in Jaime Ferrer's *Annunciation* (fig. 30).

The use of precious fabrics during the Middle Ages was not limited to the interiors of buildings. Frequently textiles were also used to adorn the street fronts of urban buildings. For festivals, processions, the reception of royalty, and other special occasions townspeople would drape the façades of their houses with decorative fabrics. A very early instance of this was recorded in the sixth century by Gregory of Tours in his account of the baptism of Clovis (reigned AD 481-511).[16] A twelfth-century German poem, Ulrich von Eschenbach's *Alexander*, had the following description of the streets of Babylon that were prepared for the entry of Alexander the Great into the city:

. . .and all the streets were hung
with large rich cloths.
The marketplace and all of their temples,
the altars and all of the shrines
were draped and adorned
with many, varied colors.
Now nothing was neglected:
in the city all the streets
were prepared with carpets,
very precious cloths were spread upon them,
they radiated a golden shine . . . .[17]

Admittedly, medieval poets often exaggerated the splendor of such occasions; the wealth and beauty of an Oriental city might be expected to call forth particularly lavish descriptions. But a description by the French four-

Figure 31. *Perugia Towel*. Self-patterned and tabby weaves. Italy, Perugia(?), ca. 1500. CMA 17.281 (cat. no. 13).

Figure 30. Jaime Ferrer II, Spanish, active mid-15th century. *The Annunciation to the Virgin*. Panel, 49 x 68 inches. Gift of Francis Ginn, Marian Ginn Jones, Barbara Ginn Griesinger, and Alexander Ginn in Memory of Frank Hadley Ginn and Cornelia Root Ginn, CMA 53.660.

Figure 32. Giovanni di Francesco Toscani, Italian, ca. 1370/80-1430. *The Race of the Palio in the Streets of Florence.* Panel from a *cassone*, ca. 1417-29. CMA 16.801 (cat. no. 22).

teenth-century chronicler Jean Froissart of a real event, the entry of Isabelle of Bavaria into Paris in 1389, recounts that the rue Saint-Denis was draped "to the skys" ("*à ciel*") with rich silks like those of Alexandria and Damascus.[18] This charming custom, so vividly described by medieval poets and chroniclers, has survived into our own time, as witnessed by the following description of the city of Warsaw prepared for the arrival of Pope John Paul II in June of 1979: "Embroidered banners and precious carpets pinned with flowers and pictures of the pope hung from the narrow windows. The slanting slate roofs unfurled long streamers in the yellow and white colors of the Vatican and the red and white colors of Poland."[19]

The practice of hanging valuable textiles from windows that faced the streets is also described in medieval poetry.[20] A colorful panel from a *cassone*, or chest, painted by Giovanni di Francesco Toscani shows that the custom was known in Florence in the early years of the fifteenth century (fig.32).[21] In fact, several fifteenth-century Florentine *cassone* panels show carpets hanging from the windows of houses.[22] In this panel, what appear to be geometrically patterned Turkish carpets, two of them with a stylized lamb motif, are shown draped over the windowsills to decorate a façade on the occasion of the annual race of the palio, part of the celebration of the feast of John the Baptist. The winner of the race will receive the palio, or banner, born on the wheeled float at the left. The palio is made of two patterned silks: one, a gold palmette design; the other, gold fleurs-de-lis on a black ground.

In another outdoor scene, represented on a panel from a fourteenth-century ivory casket, textiles are used in a similar way. In this case, large rectangles of fabric have been draped over the balconies from which a group of men and women observe a joust (fig.33). Although the unpainted ivory carving provides no clue as to the type of fabric, textiles hanging from balconies in Gothic manuscript paintings are usually patterned, often with gold, and are certainly meant to be either silks or tapestries.[23] While placing thick carpets over windowsills or smooth silks over balcony railings might have added in small measure to the comfort of those who leaned on them while witnessing the events taking place below, the

47

primary reasons for this practice must have been to enhance the festivity of the occasion and to display the wealth and good taste of the owner of the house or castle.

The horses ridden by the jousting knights on the ivory panel are caparisoned with fabric, again of unidentifiable type. The use of fine silks for horse trappings is known from descriptions in medieval literature as well as from countless depictions in medieval paintings (see fig. 28).[24] Among the elegantly caparisoned horses in Benozzo Gozzoli's fresco *The Procession of the Magi* in Florence (1459) is one wearing a rose-colored horse blanket with a pattern of gold rosettes.[25] The pattern closely resem-

bles that of a fragment of cut and voided velvet in the Cleveland Museum of Art (fig. 34). It is a brilliantly colored fabric featuring, on a white satin ground, a pile design of small floral motifs framing six-petalled rosettes. A strong Eastern influence is evident in both the color scheme and the tile-like effect of the design.[26]

Just as medieval panel and manuscript paintings reveal many ways that textiles were used both indoors and out by the affluent upper classes, paintings and other works of art also show aristocratic clothing styles in all their variety, splendor, and eccentricity. This is especially significant because relatively few pieces of secular clothing survive compared to the number of ecclesiastical

vestments that were preserved in churches. Along with descriptions in literature, inventories, and other documents, works of art are an essential resource for the study of medieval costumes. Thus a wedding portrait by an unknown south German master can be studied to determine the types of garments worn by a noble bridal couple around 1470 (fig.35). The unidentified man and woman are conservatively attired in fashions whose origins are traceable to the previous century. Certainly this is true of the man's short-skirted jacket, exaggeratedly pointed shoes, and *mi-parti* color scheme.[27] That the painting was made to commemorate the wedding of the young couple is indicated by details such as the bridal garlands adorning their heads—hers lavishly set with pearls and gemstones—and the matching wedding rings they wear. Following tradition, the bride's hair is worn long and loose to signify her maidenhood. Her lover hands her a sprig of wild chicory, a plant used in love magic, and has stuck another sprig of it in his hair.[28]

Although there was no preferred color for wedding gowns in the Middle Ages, red was frequently chosen, since it was associated with love. The costliness of scarlet-colored fabric, produced with rare and expensive dyes, enhanced the inherent brilliance and warmth of the cloth.[29] In this case the bride and groom wear matching colors—red, green, and white interrupted by a left sleeve of a brownish brocaded or damask material. The donning of a contrasting left sleeve, a fairly common practice in the later fifteenth century, here provides additional evidence that the two are betrothed. For ease of movement the lady has caught up her skirt in heavy folds in front. This pose displays her fine white underskirt and also serves to emphasize her swollen abdomen, a mark of female beauty at the time.

The composition of the painting, with the figures silhouetted against a background of dark, thick, flowering vegetation, may reflect the influence of a *mille-fleurs* tapestry such as the *Scene of Courtly Life* in the collection of the Philadelphia Museum of Art (fig. 36). The large group of *mille-fleurs*, or thousand-flowers, tapestries produced at the end of the fifteenth and beginning of the sixteenth centuries is characterized by a dark blue-green or red background filled with blossoming vegetation.[30] The splendidly garbed couple in the Philadelphia tapestry is silhouetted against this dark, lush background of flowers, among which pinks, or carnations, can be identified—

Figure 36. *Scene of Courtly Love.* Tapestry. Franco-Flemish, ca. 1490. Philadelphia Museum of Art, 26-73-1 (cat. no. 15).

Figure 35. Anonymous South German Master. *A Bridal Pair.* Panel, 14-3/8 x 24-1/2 inches (painted surface), ca. 1470. Delia E. and L.E. Holden Funds, CMA 32.179.

50

—most noticeably between the man and the woman. Since the carnation was a popular emblem of betrothal and marriage in the fifteenth scentury it is possible that the tapestry was created to commmemorate a wedding.[31]

This tapestry can be considered important not only as a prime example of the tapestry wall hangings found in stylish interiors around 1500 but also, like the German painting (fig. 35), as a detailed depiction of fashionable attire at the end of the Middle Ages. In the consideration of costumes in tapestries, however, some caution should be exercised. Because tapestry weavers often reused designs, the costumes appearing in their works are sometimes those of a previous decade. And tapestry designers frequently dressed figures in fantasy costumes more picturesque and luxurious than the real clothing of the period.[32] In this example, the attire of the elegant, aristocratic couple is that which was fashionable at the end of the fifteenth century in northern Europe.[33] The elongated silhouette of the earlier 1400s (figs. 28 and 35) has been replaced by a squarer look, noticeable in the lady's close-fitting bonnet, with its long folds of cloth (called lappets) framing the face, and in the man's cap. He wears, over stylishly long hair, a French bonnet, a low rather broadcrowned hat with an upturned brim adorned with a brooch or medallion. The V-shaped neckline of ladies' gowns of the recent past (see fig. 28) has given way to a low-cut square neckline revealing a fine linen chemise. The voluminous sleeves of the woman's

chemise are gathered at the wrist by gem-studded bracelets. Both figures wear gowns of velvet. The lady's gown features detachable sleeves tied on with ribbons so that the chemise puffs out at the shoulders, a popular conceit at the turn of the century. Her richly brocaded cloak is lined with ermine and edged with a jewelled border, probably an exaggeration of the luxuriousness of the actual clothing of the period. Her harp-strumming companion wears a less opulent overgarment, a red mantle with applied bands of ornament. His striped stockings are characteristic of fashions around 1500, as are his broad-toed shoes, a reaction against the *poulaines* worn a generation earlier.

Evidence of medieval garments and the textiles used to fashion them is also provided by sculpture from the period, especially when the original polychromy has been preserved. A pair of thirteenth-century Spanish oak statues of the mourning Virgin and St. John from a Crucifixion group have retained their original color almost intact (figs. 37, 38). Medieval artists had little knowledge of historical costumes and did not usually attempt to dress Biblical figures in "correct" clothing, portraying them instead in contemporary medieval garb. In these examples Mary and John wear almost identical costumes, since the dramatic differentiation of male and female attire was not common until the fourteenth century.[34] They are dressed in narrow, long-sleeved shifts adorned only by contrasting borders at the neck- and hemlines. Mary's

is worn over a slightly longer chemise or underdress, and a matronly veil covers her hair. Both figures are draped in mantles polychromed to imitate patterned silk with an ermine lining. The red "silk" is ornamented with a grid of diamond shapes, each containing a star-flower of either green or blue and yellow. Despite the humility and poverty attributed to these individuals in the Biblical account, the artist has dressed them in costly and sumptuous garments in recognition of their spiritual nobility.

Very similar costumes are worn by both male and female figures in an illumination from a Psalter produced by monks of Helmarshausen in Germany around 1170-90 (fig. 39). In the upper half of the image King Solomon faces a woman representing the Sponsa, or Bride, of the Song of Songs, from whom he is separated by personifications of Truth and Justice emerging from the earth and sky. Solomon and the Sponsa wear silk tunics, or shifts, over white chemises, and loosely draped mantles fastened at the neck. Decorative borders accent the hems of their shifts; a similar band marks the high waistline of the Sponsa's tunic. In the Nativity scene below, the costumes of both the scroll-bearing woman at the left and the reclining Virgin in the center also have decorative borders at the hem and/or neckline. While robes of fine silk seem appropriate for the Old Testament figures in the upper frame, the artist disregarded historical realism in portraying the Virgin clad

Figure 37. *Mourning Virgin*. Polychromed oak. Spain, Kingdom of Castile and Leon, ca. 1250-75. CMA 30.621 (cat. no. 25).

Figure 38. *Mourning St. John*. Polychromed oak. Spain, Kingdom of Castile and Leon, ca. 1250-75. CMA 30.622 (cat. no. 26).

in elegant garments sparkling with gold, and reclining on a mat of patterned silks.

Throughout the Middle Ages, as clothing styles developed and changed, ornamental borders and bands remained a popular type of trim for both ecclesiastical and aristocratic secular garments. These decorative bands might be very restrained, like the ones on the shifts of the Mourning Virgin and St. John (figs. 37, 38), or more imaginative, like those adorning the mantle of the gentleman in the *Scene of Courtly Love* (fig. 36). A fragment from a tablet-woven silk galloon, or border, in The Cleveland Museum of Art at first appears very simple with its reddish-brown and yellowish-tan stripes of varying width (fig. 40). Closer inspection reveals, however, that gold filé wefts have been superimposed over the silk to create delicate diamond and chain patterns within the stripes. This gold patterning must have rendered the border quite sumptuous when new. Another tablet-woven band with a similar striped and geometric design is attached to a crown-cap found in the tomb of Henry IV (died 1106) at Speyer It has been dated to the end of the

Figure 39. *Leaf from a Gospel Book (Trier Codex 142): The Nativity.* Manuscript illumination, 9-3/8 x 13-9/16 inches. Germany, Saxony, Helmarshausen, 1170-90. Purchase from the J.H. Wade Fund, CMA 33.445.

Figure 40. *Fragment of a Galloon.* Tablet weave. Germany(?), end of the 11th century. CMA 40.492 (cat. no. 16).

Figure 41. *Border Ornament.* Tapestry.
Italy, Lombardy(?), early 15th century.
CMA 50.3 (cat. no. 17).
See also color cover.

Figure 42. *Panel Chest.* Oak. England, late
15th-early 16th century. CMA 71.281 (cat. no. 27).

eleven century and tentatively attributed to Germany, providing some
basis for dating and localizing the
Cleveland galloon.[35]

Tablet-weaving was a widely used
technique for the creation of borders
from the ninth through the thirteenth
centuries in western and northern
Europe.[36] Done without a loom, tablet-
weaving makes use of small square or
polygonal boards with holes in the corners to hold and organize the warp for
weaving. Judging from portrayals in
medieval art of women producing borders by this method, it must have been
an aristocratic pastime as well as an
established professional craft.[37]

A tapestry band woven of polychrome
silks and silver wire on a gold ground
demonstrates the heights of artistic
and technical achievement attained in
the Gothic period in the creation of
ornamental bands and borders (fig. 41).
The three escutcheons that punctuate
the design cannot be specifically identi-

fied, but they have been linked to the Visconti family of Milan.[38] Hunting motifs fill the remaining areas of the band. They belong to a repertory of motifs, most of which originated in Italy in the fifteenth century. For example, the bristling boar flanked by two attacking dogs biting its ears can be found in a medal designed by Pisanello and in a fifteenth-century Florentine engraving in the British Museum.[39] The graphic scenes of struggle and death have been rendered beautiful by elegance of design and flawlessness of execution. This incongruous wedding of the gruesome and the splendid must have ornamented a garment worn by an Italian noblewoman, perhaps a Visconti. The band has sometimes been identified as a belt, in which case it would have been worn high under the bust without a buckle and positioned so that the shield with the lady's device was centered in the front while the ends were caught at the back.[40] Against this supposition it can be argued that

the gold wire used to weave the background makes the band too stiff to tie. Furthermore, it shows neither signs of wear from tying nor any indication that a fastener was ever attached to it, which points to the possibility that the band served as an ornamental border. It seems to be complete except for the finishing edge at the left end.

The textiles that were such an indispensable component of medieval domestic and public life—from precious hangings and clothing to tablecloths and towels—were usually stored in chests when not in use.[41] Chests were the most ubiquitous type of medieval furniture, required for the storage of all sorts of belongings. They also served as luggage for peripatetic seigneurial households moving from one manor to another and transporting large quantities of clothing and chamber textiles. English and French inventories and account books from the fourteenth and fifteenth centuries list many textiles among the contents of storage chests:

tablecloths, sheeting, clothing, hangings, layette linens, and lengths of wool, linen, and silk.[42]

Footed chests were preferable for the storage of valuable belongings, since they protected their contents from contact with damp floors. An English chest of the late fifteenth or early sixteenth century might have had this function (fig. 42). Constructed of oak, always the first choice of medieval furniture makers because of its strength and durability, the chest consists of a framework enclosing panels carved in a linenfold pattern. Linenfold decoration, so called because the shallow relief ornament resembles folded napkins, was commonly used on English furniture at the termination of the Gothic period. Although the chest's original function is unknown, perhaps the textile-inspired linenfold design designated it as a receptacle for clothing, household linens, or other domestic textiles.

1. Eames 1977, p. 229.

2. Wardwell 1983, figs. 2, 3.

3. Ibid., pp. 61-62, for the other inscriptions on the curtain.

4. Partearroyo 1977.

5. Milliken 1925, p. 70.

6. A number of other examples can be seen in a late fifteenth-century French manuscript of Jean Froissart's *Grands chroniques de France* (The British Library, Harley Ms. 4379-80). See Coulton 1930, illus. pp. 40, 60, 100, etc.

7. See Michel 1852, 1:228-30. and 2: 177-78; also Christie 1938, p. 6, on the use of fine silks for banners and horse trappings.

8. Christie 1938, p. 6.

9. Michel 1852, 2:144.

10. A remarkable instance of the survival of medieval bedcovers is the group of thirty tapestries executed around 1450 to serve as covers for the sick-beds of the hospital, the Hôtel-Dieu, at Beaune. See Weigert 1962, p. 74. For a study of beds and their furnishings in medieval Norway—with applications for other parts of Europe as well—see Hoffman 1983.

11. Michel 1852, 1:264-65; for other descriptions of bed furnishings in medieval poetry see pp. 237-38, 249, and 2:88-89.

12. See, for example, Houston 1939, pp. 135 (fig. 239), 166 (fig. 292), and Klesse 1967, pp. 471-78, cat. nos. 497-511.

13. Almost all of these symbols also appear in the Mystical Grapes tapestry (fig. 18) and have been analyzed in detail by Wardwell 1975, pp. 17-21.

14. Burnham 1980, p. 34. Such fabrics are also known as self-patterned weaves.

15. See Hartford 1952, pp. 61-62, figs. 176-77; Billeter 1966/67, p. 139; Chicago 1969, p. 63 and pl. 43; Zurich 1975, p. 29, cat. no. 21; and Geijer 1979, p. 171. Errera 1921, p. 150, cites a Sienese inventory of 1482 that lists three altar cloths from Perugia with a design of dragons and lions woven in cotton.

16. Kurth 1926, 1:16.

17. Ulrich von Eschenbach, 1888 ed., vv. 14483-90. The translation is my own. I wish to thank Professor Petrus Tax of the University of North Carolina, Chapel Hill, for his helpful suggestions.

18. Michel 1852, 2:42.

19. "Poles greet pope with display of loyalty," *Raleigh News and Observer*, June 3, 1979.

20. Michel 1852, 2:129-30.

21. In 1943 Iris Origo observed Italian villagers carrying on this venerable tradition in celebration of a rumored armistice: "At Pontassieve flags and carpets were hanging from the windows" (Origo 1984, p. 59).

22. London 1983, pp. 10 (illus.), 11, 14; John Mills identifies the carpets represented in the *cassone* panels as either simplifed versions of Turkish rugs or Italian-made imitations of them.

23. See, for example, the *mille-fleurs* tapestry hung from an indoor balcony in a miniature in Froissart's *Grands chroniques de France*, illustrated in Coulton 1930, pl. V.

24. See note 7 above and Coulton 1930, pls. I, II, and illus. pp. 12, 13, 28, etc.

25. For an illustration of this detail of Gozzoli's fresco in the Palazzo Medici-Riccardi, see Toesca 1958, pl. XIX.

26. Davison 1942, p. 21.

27. See Payne 1965, pp. 177-97, 228.

28. On medieval betrothal and marriage customs see Gautier 1959, pp. 157-95; Denecke 1971; and Murstein 1974, pp. 139-42.

29. On medieval scarlet, a particular type of fine wool fabric that might or might not be scarlet-colored, and for a discussion of red dyes, see Munro 1983.

30. For an overview of the most important *mille-fleurs* tapestries see Weigert 1962, pp. 76-82. Traditionally the *mille-fleurs* tapestries have been attributed to itinerant weavers in the Loire Valley of France, but the consensus of recent scholarship rejects the Loire Valley attribution in favor of an attribution to ateliers in Flanders or in the Burgundian Lowlands. The most extensive arguments have been made by Sophie Schneebalg-Perelman in favor of Brussels as their place of manufacture. For a summary of earlier attributions and her own reasons for favoring Brussels, see Schneebalg-Perelman 1967. A concise English summary of the debate can be found in Freeman 1976, pp. 212-17.

31. On the symbolism of carnations see Freeman 1976, pp. 144-47.

32. Evans 1952, p. 66.

33. On late fifteenth-century fashions see Houston 1939, pp. 177-98; Evans 1952, pp. 59-66; and Payne 1965, pp. 199-259.

34. On costumes of the twelfth and thirteenth centuries see Houston 1939, pp. 41-53; Evans 1952, pp. 1-25; and Payne 1965, pp. 157-75.

35. Kubach and Haas 1972, 1: 949-50, and 2: fig. 1482.

36. Schuette 1956.

37. Wyss 1973, figs. 15, 17, 20-22, 25.

38. The shield at each end bears a red and silver eagle on an opposing silver and red ground, but the Visconti eagle is black on a gold ground. The shield in the center with a serpent on the sinister and a castle and vair on the quartered dexter has been identified as belonging to a married female member of the Visconti family, but which one remains undetermined. (Information from unpublished notes in the curator's file of the Textile Department of The Cleveland Museum of Art.)

39. Illustrated by Van Marle 1931, 1: figs. 245-47. Other hunt motifs found on the tapestry band and in fifteenth-century Italian art are discussed and illustrated in Van Marle 1931, 1: 248-54; see also Degenhart and Schmitt 1968, 1/1: 256-63, cat. nos. 154-55, and 1/3: pls. 185-90.

40. New York 1975, p. 79, cat. no. 86.

41. For a thorough discussion of medieval chests see Eames 1977, pp.108-40; see also London 1923, pp. 12-14, p. 53, cat. no. 299, and pl. 45.

42. See Eames 1977, pp. 122-26, for the pertinent inventories.

Catalogue

References cited under the bibliography for the individual objects are those that were found to be the most useful for the preparation of the preceding text material. In abbreviated form here, they appear as full citations in the Selected Bibliography at the back of the book.

TEXTILES

1 Back of a Chasuble with Orphrey Cross

The Madonna and Child (top center), Saints Catherine (left), Dorothy (right), Ursula (middle center), and Barbara (bottom).

(a) Chasuble: cut and voided polychrome silk velvet with pomegranate pattern, 43-3/8 x 26-1/2 inches overall. Italy, early 15th century.

(b) Orphrey cross: embroidery of polychrome silks and gold filé on linen. Bohemia, 15th century.

Purchase from the J. H. Wade Fund
CMA 50.85

Bibliography: Svec 1952; Chicago 1975, cat. no. 25 (with additional bibliography).

See Figure 2.

2 Fragment of a Chasuble with Orphrey Cross

(a) Chasuble: lampas weave of tan silk (originally red) and membrane gold (gilt has worn off), 27-1/2 x 41-7/8 inches overall. Italy, last third of the 14th century.

(b) Orphrey cross: compound twill weave of linen, polychrome silks, and gold filé. Germany, Cologne, 14th century.

(c) Embroidered bands bordering orphreys: solid cut blue velvet of silk and linen, embroidered with polychrome silks and gold filé, W. 1 inch. Germany, Cologne, 14th century.

Purchase from the J.H. Wade Fund
CMA 28.653

Bibliography: Underhill 1929; Baltimore 1962, cat. no. 157 (with additional bibliography); Chicago 1975, cat. no. 12 (with additional bibliography); Wardwell 1976/77, pp. 200-202.

See Figure 3 and Color Plate I.

3 Orphrey Panel with the Tree of Jesse

Top to bottom: Achim, Ezechias-Rex, and Eliud.

Embroidery in polychrome silks, gold filé, and silver(?) filé on a double layer of linen, 6-5/8 x 39 inches. England, third quarter of the 14th century.

Purchase from the J.H. Wade Fund CMA 49.503

Bibliography: Riefstahl 1950; Shepherd 1950; Chicago 1975, cat. no. 14 (with additional bibliography).

See Figure 4.

4 The Madonna and Child with Saints

Left to right: St. Catherine, St. John the Evangelist, the Madonna and Child, St. Jodokus, and St. Mary Magdalene.

Tapestry of polychrome wools and silks on an undyed linen warp, 38 x 72 inches. Germany, Nuremburg, ca. 1490.

Gift of Leonard C. Hanna, Jr., for the Coralie Walker Hanna Memorial Collection CMA 39.162

Bibliography: Kurth 1926, 1:189, 273; Luitpold (Herzog in Bayern) 1926, pp. 79-80; Göbel 1933, 3/1:173-74.

See Figure 6 and Color Plate II.

5 The Coronation of the Virgin

Saints Verdiana (left) and Anthony Abbot (right) and angels.

Embroidery of polychrome silks, gold filé, and silver filé on linen (figures embroidered separately, backed with paper, then applied to the tondo), diam. 22-3/4 inches. Italy, Florence, first half of the 15th century; design attributed to Paolo Schiavo.

Purchase from the J. H. Wade Fund CMA 53.129

Bibliography: Shepherd 1954; Baltimore 1962, cat. no. 159 (with additional bibliography); Degenhart and Schmitt 1968, 1/2: cat. no. 346.

See Figure 7 and Color Plate III.

6 Scenes from the Life of the Virgin

Left to right: The Annunciation, the Nativity, the Adoration of the Magi, the Presentation in the Temple, Christ among the Doctors, and the Assumption of the Virgin.

Embroidery of polychrome silks, gold filé, and silver filé on a double layer of linen, 6-1/4 x 49-3/4 inches (embroidered surface). Italy, Florence, first third of the 14th century.

Andrew R. and Martha Holden Jennings Fund   CMA 78.36

Bibliography: Wardwell 1979 (with additional bibliography).

See Figure 11.

7 Fragment with the Annunciation to Mary

Lampas weave of blue and white silks and membrane gold, 9-1/16 x 18-1/2 inches. Italy, last third of the 14th century.

Dudley P. Allen Fund CMA 31.61

Bibliography: Underhill 1931; Wardwell 1976/77, pp. 189-91.

See Figure 15.

8 Fragment of a Woven Bag

Above, alternately: the arms of De Châtillon, count of Blois, and of France. Below, alternately: the arms of Flanders and De Dreux, duke of Brittany.

Tapestry weave of polychrome silks and gold filé, 4-3/4 x 7-1/4 inches. France, second half of the 13th century.

Purchase from the J. H. Wade Fund CMA 39.37

Bibliography: Underhill 1939; Hartford 1952, cat. no. 67 (with additional bibliography).

See Figure 16.

9 Reliquary Bag

Compound twill weave of blue and tan silk, 13-1/8 x 14-1/8 inches. Spain, Mudejar(?), 13th century.

Purchase from the J. H. Wade Fund CMA 74.101

Bibliography: CMA Bulletin 62 (1975): 102, no. 149 (illus.).

See Figure 17.

10 The Mystical Grapes

Tapestry of polychrome wools and silks and gold filé (gilt has worn off) on undyed wool warps, 28-7/8 x 27-7/8 inches (as framed). Flanders, ca. 1500.

Purchase, John L. Severance Fund CMA 73.77

Bibliography: Wardwell 1975.

See Figure 18.

11 Mantle for a Statue of the Virgin

Lampas weave of polychrome silks, 41 x 85 inches. Spain, Hispano-Islamcic, 15th century.

Purchase from the J. H. Wade Fund CMA 29.975

Bibliography: Underhill 1930; May 1957, p. 156.

See Figure 22.

12 Roundels with Scenes of the Celestial Banquet and Hunt

Tapestry of polychrome silks and membrane gold inwoven in a red silk fabric of tabby weave, 7-3/8 x 22-5/8 inches. Spain, Hispano-Islamic, probably Almeria, first half of the 13th century.

Purchase from the J. H. Wade Fund CMA 66.368

Bibliography: Shepherd 1978 (with additional bibliography).

See Figure 23.

13 Perugia Towel

White areas: cotton, self-patterned weaves. Solid blue bands: weft-faced tabby. Figured bands: tabby with supplementary pattern weft, 20 x 42-1/2 inches. Italy, Perugia (?), ca. 1500.

Gift of Miss Caroline F. Coit CMA 17.281

Unpublished.

See Figure 31.

14 Fragment of Velvet

Cut and voided velvet of polychrome silks, 9-1/2 x 15-1/8 inches. Italy, 15th century.

Dudley P. Allen Fund CMA 18.310

Bibliography: Los Angeles 1944.

See Figure 34.

15 Scene of Courtly Love

Tapestry of polychrome wools and silks on an undyed wool warp, 63-1/2 x 97 inches. Franco-Flemish, ca. 1490.

Philadelphia Museum of Art, 26-73-1.

Bibliography: Downs 1927; Göbel 1928, 2/1:280.

See Figure 36.

16 Fragment of a Galloon

Tablet weave of polychrome silk and gold filé (band woven with over 246 tablets in quarter turns throughout), 2-3/4 x 13-1/2 inches. Germany (?), end of the 11th century.

Dudley P. Allen Fund CMA 40.492

Unpublished.

See Figure 40.

17 Border Ornament

Tapestry of polychrome silks, gold wire, and silver wire, 3 x 36-3/4 inches. Italy, Lombardy (?), early 15th century.

Purchase from the J. H. Wade Fund CMA 50.3

Bibliography: New York 1975.

See Figure 41.

PAINTINGS

18 Madonna and Child
Follower of Hans Memling

Oil and tempera on oak panel, 8-7/16 x 12-5/16 inches (painted surface). Netherlands, Bruges, ca. 1485-90.

Delia and L. E. Holden Funds CMA 34.29

Bibliography: Cleveland 1974, cat. no. 55 (with additional bibliography).

See Figure 19.

19 The Virgin Mary Crowned by Angels
Attributed to Stephan Lochner

Oil on fir panel, 19-7/8 x 11-1/2 inches. Germany, Cologne (?), ca. 1441.

Purchase, John L. Severance Fund CMA 68.20

Bibliography: Stechow 1968; Cleveland 1974, cat. no. 9 (with additional bibliography).

See Figure 20.

20 Accidia and Her Court

Single leaf from a treatise on the vices, tempera and gold leaf on parchment, 7-1/2 x 4-1/16 inches. Italy, Genoa, or Naples (?), late 14th century.

Purchase from the J. H. Wade Fund CMA 53.152

Bibliography: Baltimore 1962, cat. no. 72.

See Figure 27 and Color Plate IV.

21 Queen Medusa Enthroned
Close to Maître François

Single leaf from a manuscript of Boccacio's *Des cleres et nobles femmes* (now Spencer MS. 33, New York Public Library), tempera and gold leaf on vellum, 5-1/8 x 3-9/16 inches. France, ca. 1470.

Gift of J. H. Wade CMA 24.1015

Bibliography: Baltimore 1949, cat. no. 110; Cleveland 1967, cat. no. VII, 5.

See Figure 28.

22 The Race of the Palio
    in the Streets of Florence
Giovanni di Francesco Toscani
(Master of the Griggs Crucifixion)

Cassone panel: oil and tempera on poplar panel, 16-9/16 x 54-7/8 inches. Italy, Florence, ca. 1417-29

The Holden Collection CMA 16.801

Bibliography: Cleveland 1974, cat. no. 45 (with additional bibliography)

See Figure 32.

MISCELLANEOUS OBJECTS

23 *The Madonna Enthroned with Eight Angels*
Master E. S.

Engraving, 4-5/16 x 6 inches, dated 1467. Germany, Upper Rhine region.

Purchase, John L. Severance Fund
CMA 48.170

Bibliography: Lehrs 1910, 2:cat. no. 76, pl. 90, no. 233 (with additional bibliography); Philadelphia 1967, cat. no. 77.

See Figure 21.

24 *Panel from a Casket (Lid)*

The seige of the Castle of Love, and a joust. Ivory, 5-1/8 x 10-3/8 inches. Franco-German, Lorraine or Lower Rhine, first half of the 14th century.

Purchase, John L. Severance Fund
CMA 78.39

Bibliography: Wixom 1979 (with additional bibliography).

See Figure 33.

25 *Mourning Virgin*

Polychromed oak, H. 61 inches. Spain, Kingdom of Castile and Leon, ca. 1250-75.

Gift of Mr. and Mrs. Francis F. Prentiss
CMA 30.621

Bibliography: Cook and Ricart 1950, p. 370.

See Figure 37.

26 *Mourning St. John*

Polychromed oak, H. 59-1/2 inches. Spain, Kingdom of Castile and Leon, ca. 1250-75.

Gift of Mr. and Mrs. Francis F. Prentiss
CMA 30.622

Bibliography: Cook and Ricart 1950, p. 370.

See Figure 38.

27 *Panel Chest*

Oak with iron hardware, 27-3/8 x 50 x 16-1/8 inches. England, late 15th-early 16th century.

Gift of Dr. and Mrs. Paul G. Ecker in memory of Dr. and Mrs. Enrique E. Ecker
CMA 71.281

Bibliography: CMA *Bulletin* 60 (1973):107, no. 49 (illus.).

See Figure 42.

Glossary

Italicized terms within definitiions are also defined in the glossary.

Alb. An ankle-length white linen undergarment with long sleeves worn by deacons, priests, and bishops under their *vestments* and by choristers, acolytes, and sub-deacons as their principal garment.

Altar cloth. A rectangular piece of white linen used to cover the top of an altar.

Altar frontal. A decoration for the front of an altar, which may be of metal, wood, or fabric. See also *antependium.*

Antependium (plural: *antependia*). A Latin term used since the late Middle Ages for an *altar frontal* of any material.

Aumônières. A French term for an alms bag; a fabric purse, usually of trapezoid shape with rounded upper corners and a flap closure, originally used to carry alms for distribution to the poor.

Brocade. In general a term used to describe any rich figured textile, especially one with a raised pattern in gold or silver. When used as a verb the term has a specific meaning: to introduce a supplementary *weft* (brocading weft) into the ground weave by means of a pointed bobbin, which moves back and forth only within the area where a particular color is required by the pattern. Because the brocading weft does not run across the entire width of the textile, this technique is used to conserve expensive *metallic thread* and to reduce the stiffness and weight of the textile.

Caparison. An ornamental covering for a horse.

Chasuble. The outer garment worn by a priest celebrating the Eucharist, usually made of fine material and decorated with *orphreys.*

Chemise. A simple slip-on shift-like garment with or without sleeves, made of lightweight material and worn as an undergarment.

Cloth of honor. A curtain of precious fabric hung or held behind a saint as a sign of holiness.

Compound twill weave. A weave combining the characteristics of *compound weave* and *twill weave.*

Compound weave. A weave in which the *weft* threads of a desired color are bound on the surface of the fabric, while the weft threads of other colors are bound on the reverse side until they are needed for the design. *Warp* threads known as "inner warps" lie between the weft threads on

61

the surface and those on the reverse in order to keep them separate. This weave results in a uniform texture and surface structure throughout the fabric.

Cope. A semicircular cape with an ornamental hood worn as a processional garment in a liturgical service. Draped over the shoulders, it is fastened across the chest with a strip of material or brooch.

Couching. A technique employing two threads, one that is laid on top of the material to be embroidered and a second used to fasten it down.

Surface couching. A technique whereby one thread is arranged in parallel rows on an area to be embroidered and a second thread is used to fasten it each time it turns upon reaching the edge of this area, as well as at intervals along its length. The second thread is looped over the first so that it is visible on the surface of the embroidery. Used in the *or nué* technique.

Underside couching. One thread is laid in parallel rows on an area to be embroidered, then, at intervals, is pulled through the ground fabric in loops and is secured on the underside by a linen thread. Thus the second, or fastening, thread is not visible on the surface of the embroidery. Used extensively in *opus anglicanum.*

Cut velvet. See *velvet.*

Dalmatic. A shin-length tunic open at the sides and with sleeves of rectangular shape, worn by deacons as their principal garment and by priests and bishops underneath the *chasuble.*

Damask. A reversible fabric in which the background and pattern, usually of a single color, are woven of two different weaves so that the pattern is visible due to the fact that light affects the weaves differently.

Drawloom. A loom for hand-weaving figured textiles, equipped with a device called a figure harness that contols some or all of the *warp* threads, making possible the regular repetition of the pattern.

Embroidery. The process of decorating a finished piece of cloth with the needle and thread.

Galloon. Trim for a garment in the form of a band, usually of rich material.

Gold filé. A type of gold thread made by wrapping strips of gilded silver around a silk core, usually yellow.

Half-silk. Fabric woven of silk and linen.

Lampas weave. A weave in which the background is formed by the main *warps* and *wefts*, while the pattern is formed by weft floats secured by a binding warp. In other words, one set of warps and wefts forms the background while another set forms the pattern. The variation in weave between these areas causes them to reflect light differently and have different textures.

Lenten cloth. A curtain hung in front of the high altar in a church to hide it from the view of the congregation during Lent.

Membrane gold. A type of gold thread made by wrapping strips of gilded animal skin or gut around a core of linen or silk. Also called Cyprian gold because this thread was manufactured in Cyprus, among other places.

Metallic thread. A term encompassing several types of gold and silver threads. See *gold filé, silver file,* and *membrane gold.*

Mille-fleurs. A French term meaning a thousand flowers; used to designate a group of tapestries woven in the fifteenth and early sixteenth centuries and characterized by a red or dark blue-green background densely scattered with woven flowers.

Mi-parti. The descriptive term for clothing that is one color on one side and a contrasting color on the other.

Moiré. The French term used to describe certain ribbed fabrics in which a rippled or watered effect is produced by pressing the ribs so as to flatten some of them and leave the rest in relief. The flattened and unflattened areas reflect light differently.

Opus anglicanum. A Latin term meaning English work; used since the Middle Ages for embroidery, primarily of silk, made in England from the twelfth to the sixteenth century.

Opus florentinum. A Latin term meaning Florentine work; used since the Middle Ages for embroidery of silk and gold made in Florence in the fourteenth and fifteenth centuries.

Opus teutonicum. A Latin term meaning German work; used since the Middle Ages for *whitework embroidery* from Germany.

Or nué. A French term meaning shaded gold; used to describe a type of *surface couching:* gold filé thread laid down in parallel lines from side to side of an area to be embroidered is fastened with a stitch each time it turns on reaching the outline. The gold is then shaded with polychrome silks. In the shaded areas of the design the colored silk couching stitches are worked so thickly that the gold is almost hidden, while in lighter areas the intervals between stitches are gradually increased until, in the highlights, the gold is exposed in all its brilliance.

Orphrey. An ornamental border or band on an ecclesiastical *vestment,* often embroidered.

Poulaines. A French term used for shoes with long pointed toes made of soft leather or fabric with leather soles; worn by fashionable men in the fourteenth and fifteenth centuries. So called because they supposedly originated in Poland.

Reliquary bag. A fabric bag used to contain sacred relics.

Satin weave. An irregular *twill weave* in which the *weft* threads disappear beneath the finer and more numerous *warp* threads, or vice versa, resulting in a smooth, glossy surface.

Self-patterned weave. A weave in which the same type of threads, often a single color, are used to weave both the background and the pattern, so that the pattern is visible due to variations in the weave

between it and the background. *Damask* is
a type of self-patterned weave.

Silver filé. Silver thread made by wrapping
strips of silver around a silk core, usually
white.

Solid velvet. See *velvet*.

Split stitch. An embroidery stitch worked in
untwisted silk thread whereby the needle
goes back slightly after each stitch to
pierce (split) the previous stitch before
continuing. Particularly useful for curved
lines, but also used to fill in large areas.

Superfrontal. A narrow band of fabric, often
embroidered and edged with fringe, sewn
to a textile *antependium* along its entire
upper length.

Surface couching. See *couching*.

Surplice. A white ecclesiastical outer
garment usually of linen, having loose
sleeves and gathered at the neck.

Tabby weave. The simplest of weaves, based
on the regular interweaving of *warps* and
wefts on the principle of under one and
over one, under one and over one, etc.

Tablet weave. A weave in which the sheds
(openings in the *warp* through which the
weft threads pass) are formed by rotating
a series of wooden tablets with holes
through which the warp threads have
been threaded. Because the number of
warp threads is limited by the number of
tablets that can conveniently be maneu-
vered, this method is normally used for
narrow bands of fabric.

Taffeta. A fine silk fabric of *tabby weave*.

Tapestry. A variation of *tabby weave* in
which colored *weft* threads are beaten
down with a comb-like beater to completely cover the undyed *warp* threads,
which are then visible only as ribs. It
differs from other weaves in that the weft
threads are not interwoven across the
entire width of the warp. Rather, the
weaver passes a weft thread back and
forth through the warps only where a
particular color is needed, using a different bobbin of thread for each color.

Twill weave. A weave based on the interweaving of *warp* and *weft* to produce
unbroken diagonal ribs. Each weft thread
passes in echelon under one or more and
over two or more (or over one or more and
under two or more) warp threads. This
produces a heavier, stronger cloth than
tabby weave.

Underside couching. See *couching*.

Velvet. A pile weave consisting of a founda-
tion weave with an extra *warp* woven
over metal rods. When the rods are with-
drawn, tiny loops of thread remain, stand-
ing up from the ground to produce the
pile.

Cut velvet. Results when grooved rods are
used so that the loops can be cut by pul-
ling a sharp tool along these grooves.

Solid velvet. A type of velvet in which the
entire surface is covered with cut pile.

Voided velvet. A velvet having certain
areas that are left free of pile by the expe-
dient of weaving the pile warp in with the
ground weave in these areas rather than
over the rods that produce the pile loops.

Vestment. One of the insignia or articles of
clothing worn by clergymen and their
assistants when officiating in church
services. Each vestment is appropriate to
the rank of the wearer and the rite being
celebrated.

Voided velvet. See *velvet*.

Warp. Those threads of a textile that are
arranged longitudinally on the loom pre-
paratory to weaving.

Weft. The transverse threads that are interwoven with the warp to create the fabric.

Weft-faced tabby. A *tabby weave* in which
the *weft* predominates, more or less con-
cealing the *warp*.

Whitework embroidery. Needlework done
in the Middle Ages by German nuns using
primarily white linen thread on a white
linen ground fabric.

Selected
Bibliography

Aldenkirchen, J. 1885. "Früh-mittel-alterliche Leinen-Stickereien." *Jahrbücher des Vereins von Alterthums-freunden im Rheinlande* 79:256-65.

Baltimore 1949. The Walters Art Gallery. *Illuminated Books of the Middle Ages and Renaissance.* Exh. cat.

Baltimore 1962. The Walters Art Gallery. *The International Style: The Arts in Europe around 1400.* Exh. cat.

Braun, Joseph. 1924a. *Der christliche Altar in seiner geschichtlichen Entwicklung.* 2 vols. Munich: G. Koch und Co.

Braun 1924b. *Die liturgischen Paramente in Gegenwart und Vergangenheit: Ein Handbuch der Paramentik.* Freiburg i. Br.: Herder und Co.

Braun 1937. "Altarantependium." In *Reallexikon zur deutschen Kunstgeschichte,* edited by Otto Schmitt, 1:441-59. Stuttgart: J.B. Metzler.

Braun 1943. *Tracht und Attribute der Heiligen in der deutschen Kunst.* Stuttgart: J. B. Metzler.

Burnham, Dorothy. 1980. *Warp and Weft: A Textile Terminology.* Toronto: Royal Ontario Museum.

Cavallo, Adolph. 1960. "A Newly Discovered Trecento Orphrey from Florence." *The Burlington Magazine* 102:505-10.

Cennini, Cennino d'Andrea. 1960. *The Craftsman's Handbook: The Italian "Il libro dell'arte."* Translated by Daniel V. Thompson. New York: Dover Publications.

Chicago 1969. The Art Institute of Chicago. *Masterpieces of Western Textiles from the Art Institute of Chicago.* Exh. cat. by Christa C. Mayer.

Chicago 1975. The Art Institute of Chicago. *Raiment for the Lord's Service: A Thousand Years of Western Vestments.* Exh. cat. by Christa C. Mayer-Thurman.

Christie, A. G. I. 1914. "The Tree of Jesse in Medieval Embroidery." *Needle and Thread* 111:18-24, 77-82.

Christie 1938. *English Medieval Embroidery.* Oxford: Clarendon Press.

Cleveland 1967. The Cleveland Museum of Art. *Treasures from Medieval France.* Exh. cat. by William D. Wixom.

Cleveland 1974. The Cleveland Museum of Art. *European Paintings Before 1500.* Catalogue of Paintings, Part 1. Coll. cat. by Ann Tzeutschler Lurie, et al.

Cleveland 1984. The Cleveland Museum of Art. *Material Matters: Fifty Years of Gifts from the Textile Arts Club.* Exh. cat. by Anne E. Wardwell.

Cole, Alan S. 1899. *Ornament in European Silks.* London: Debenham and Freebody.

Cologne 1926. Schnütgen-Museum. *Die liturgischen Gewänder und kirchlichen Stickereien des Schnütgenmuseums Köln.* Coll. cat. by Fritz Witte.

Cologne 1976. Kunstgewerbemuseum der Stadt Köln. *Europäische Seidengewebe des 13.-18. Jahrhunderts.* Kataloge des Kunstgewerbemuseums Köln, Vol. 8. Coll. cat. by Barbara Markowsky.

Cologne 1982. Schnütgen-Museum. *Messe Gregors des Grossen: Vision. Kunst. Realität.* Exh. cat. by Uwe Westfehling.

Cook, Walter W. S., and Ricart, José Guidol. 1950. *Pintura e Imagineria Romanicas.* Ars Hispaniae, vol. 6. Madrid: Editorial Plus-ultra.

Coulton, G. G. 1980. *The Chronicler of European Chivalry.* New York: Albert and Charles Boni.

Davison, Mildred. 1942. "An Exhibition of Early Velvets from the Museum Collection." *Bulletin of the Art Institute of Chicago* 36:21-22.

Degenhart, Bernhard, and Schmitt, Annegrit. 1968-82. *Corpus der italienischen Zeichnungen 1300-1450.* 8 vols. Berlin: Gebr. Mann Verlag.

Dehaisnes, Chrétien C. A. 1886. *Documents et extraits divers concernant l'histoire de l'art dans la Flandre, l'Artois et le Hainaut avant le XVe siècle.* 3 vols. Lille: L. Danel.

Deneke, Bernward. 1971. *Hochzeit.* Munich: Prestel-Verlag.

Detroit 1959. Detroit Institute of Arts. *Decorative Arts of the Italian Renaissance, 1400-1600.* Exh. cat.

De Winter, Patrick M. *See* under W.

Downs, Joseph. 1927. "An Exhibition of Tapestries." *The Pennsylvania Museum Bulletin* 22:309-14.

Eames, Penelope. 1977. *Furniture in England, France, and the Netherlands from the Twelfth to the Fifteenth Century.* Vol. 13 of *Furniture History* (The Journal of the Furniture History Society).

Engelmeier, Paul. 1961. *Westfälische Hungertücher vom 14. bis 19. Jahrhundert.* Münster: Verlag Aschendorff.

Errera, Isabelle. 1921. "Les tissus reproduits sur les tableaux italiens du XIVe au XVIIe siècle." *Gazette des Beaux-Arts* ser. 5, 4:143-58.

Evans, Joan. 1952. *Dress in Medieval France.* Oxford: Clarendon Press.

Falke, Otto von, et al. 1930. *The Guelph Treasure: The Sacred Relics of Brunswick Cathedral.* Translated by Silvia M. Welsch. Frankfurt: Frankfurter Verlags-Anstalt.

Freeman, Margaret B. 1976. *The Unicorn Tapestries.* New York: The Metropolitan Museum of Art.

Fremantle, Richard. 1975. *Florentine Gothic Painters from Giotto to Masaccio: A Guide to Painting in and near Florence 1300-1450.* London: Martin Secker and Warburg.

Gautier, Leon. 1959. *La Chevalerie.* Paris: Jacques Levron.

Gay, Victor. 1887-1928. *Glossaire archéologique du Moyen-Age et de la Renaissance.* 2 vols. Paris: Librairie de la société bibliographique.

Geijer, Agnes. 1979. *A History of Textile Art.* London: Pasold Research Fund in association with Sotheby Parke Bernet Publications.

Göbel, Heinrich. 1928. *Wandteppiche.* Vol. 2, *Die romanischen Länder.* Leipzig: Klinkhardt und Biermann.

Göbel, Heinrich. 1933. *Wandteppiche.* Vol. 3, pt. 1, *Die germanischen und slawischen Länder.* Berlin: Klinkhardt und Biermann.

Gravenkamp, C. 1967. "Antependium." In *Lexikon der Marienkunde*, edited by Konrad Algermissen, 1:272-75. Regensburg: Verlag Friedrich Pustet.

Grönwoldt, Ruth. 1961. "Florentiner Stickereien in den Inventaren des Herzogs von Berry und der Herzöge von Burgund." *Mitteilungen des Kunsthistorischen Institutes in Florenz* 10:33-58.

Grönwoldt 1968. "Paramente und ihre Stifter: Italienische Paramente des Trecento in zwei französischen Kathedralen." In *Festschrift Ulrich Middeldorf,* edited by Antje Kosegarten and Peter Tigler, pp. 81-87. Berlin: Walter de Gruyter und Co.

Grönwoldt 1969. "A Florentine Fourteenth-Century Ophrey in the Toledo Museum of Art." *Apollo* 89:350-55.

Guldan, Ernst. 1966. *Eva und Marie: Eine Antithese als Bildmotiv.* Graz-Cologne: Hermann Böhlaus Nachfolger.

Hartford 1952. The Wadsworth Atheneum. *2000 Years of Tapestry Weaving: A Loan Exhibition.* Exh. cat. by Adèle Coulin Weibel.

Hayward, Jane. 1971. "Sacred Vestments as They Developed in the Middle Ages." *The Bulletin of the Metropolitan Museum of Art* n.s. 29:300-309.

Hoffman, Marta. 1983. "Beds and Bedclothes in Medieval Norway." In *Cloth and Clothing in Medieval Europe: Essays in Memory of Professor E. M. Carus-Wilson,* edited by N. B. Harte and K. G. Ponting, pp. 351-67. London: Heinemann Educational Books for the Pasold Research Fund.

Houston, Mary G. 1939. *Medieval Costume in England and France: The 13th, 14th and 15th Centuries.* London: Adam and Charles Black.

Katzenellenbogen, Adolf. 1964. *The Sculptural Programs of Chartres Cathedral.* New York: W. W. Norton.

King, Donald. 1965. "A Venetian Embroidered Altar Frontal. "*Victoria and Albert Museum Bulletin* 1:15-25.

Klesse, Brigitte. 1960. "Darstellung von Seidenstoffen in der altkölner Malerei." In *Mouseion: Studien aus Kunst und Geschichte für Otto H. Foerster,* edited by Heinz Ladendorf, et al., pp. 217-25. Cologne: M. DuMont Schauberg.

Klesse 1967. *Seidenstoffe in der italienischen Malerei des 14. Jahrhunderts.* Bern: Schriften der Abegg-Stiftung Bern im Verlag Stämpfli und Cie.

Kroos, Renate. 1970. *Niedersächische Bildstickerein des Mittelalters.* Berlin: Deutscher Verlag für Kunstwissenschaft.

Kubach, Hans Erich, and Haas, Walter. 1972. *Der Dom zur Speyer.* 2 vols. Die Kunstdenkmäler von Rheinland-Pfalz, vol. 5. Munich: Deutscher Kunstverlag.

Kurth, Betty. 1926. *Die deutschen Bildteppiche des Mittelalters.* 3 vols. Vienna: Anton Schroll.

Kurth 1931. "Florentiner Trecento-Stickereien." *Pantheon* 8:455-62.

Lehrs, Max. 1910. *Geschichte und kritischer Katalog des deutschen, niederländischen und französischen Kupferstichs im XV. Jahrhundert.* Vol. 2, *Der Meister E. S.* Vienna: Gesellschaft für Vervielfältigende Kunst.

London 1923. Victoria and Albert Museum. *Gothic and Early Tudor.* Catalogue of English Furniture and Woodwork, Vol. 1. Coll cat. by H. Clifford Smith.

London 1983. National Gallery. *Carpets in Paintings.* Exh. cat. by John Mills.

Longhi, Roberto. 1940. "Paolo Schiavo." *La critica d'arte* 5, no. 25-26, pt. 2:187-89.

Los Angeles 1944. Los Angeles County Museum. *2000 Years of Silk Weaving.* Exh. cat. with intro. by Adèle Coulin Weibel.

Luitpold (Herzog in Bayern) 1926. *Die fränkische Bildwirkerei.* 2 vols. Munich: Kurt Wolff.

Mâle, Emile. 1972. *The Gothic Image: Religious Art in France of the Thirteenth Century.* Translated by Dora Nussey. New York: Harper and Row.

Markowsky, Barbara. 1973. "Eine Gruppe bemalter Paliotti in Florenz und der Toskana und ihre Textilen Vorbilder." *Mitteilungen des Kunsthistorischen Institutes in Florence* 17:105-40.

Marle, Raimond van. 1931-32. *Iconographie de l'art profane au Moyen-age et à la Renaissance.* 2 vols. The Hague: Martinus Nijhoff.

May, Florence Lewis. 1957. *Silk Textiles of Spain.* New York: Hispanic Society of America.

Mayer-Thurman, Christa C. 1975. "The Significance of Mass Vestments." *Art and Artists* 10:14-21.

Metford, J. C. J. 1983. *Dictionary of Christian Lore and Legend.* London: Thames and Hudson.

Michel, Francisque Xavier. 1852-54. *Recherches sur le commerce, la fabrication, et l'usage des étoffes de soie, d'or et d'argent, et autres tissues précieux en Occident, principalement en France, pendant le moyen âge.* 2 vols. Paris: Crapelet.

Milliken, William M. 1975. "Illuminated Miniatures in The Cleveland Museum of Art." *The Bulletin of The Cleveland Museum of Art* 12:61-72.

Müller, Johanna. 1944. "Das Zehdenicker Fastentuch." *Marburger Jahrbuch für Kunstwissenschaft* 13:103-10

Munich 1955. Bayerisches Nationalmuseum. *Sakrale Gewänder des Mittalalters.* Exh. cat. by Sigrid Müller-Christensen.

Munro, John H. 1983. "The Medieval Scarlet and the Economics of Sartorial Splendour." In *Cloth and Clothing in Medieval Europe: Essay in Memory of Professor E. M. Carus-Wilson.* edited by N. B. Harte and K. G. Ponting, pp. 13-70. London: Heinemann Educational Books for the Pasold Research Fund.

Murstein, Bernard I. 1974. *Love, Sex, and Marriage through the Ages.* New York: Springer Publishing Co.

New York 1975. The Metropolitan Museum of Art. *The Secular Spirit: Life and Art at the End of the Middle Ages.* Exh. cat. by Timothy Husband and Jane Hayward.

Origo, Iris 1984. *War in Val d'Orcia: An Italian War Diary 1943-1944.* Boston: David R. Godine.

Panofsky, Erwin, ed.1946. *Abbot Suger on the Abbey Church of St.-Denis and Its Art Treasures.* Princeton: Princeton Univ. Press.

Partearroyo, Cristina. 1977. "Spanish-Moslem Textile." *Bulletin de Liaison du Centre International d'Etude des Textiles Anciens* 45:78-81.

Payne, Blanche. 1965. *History of Costume from the Ancient Egyptians to the Twentieth Century.* New York: Harper and Row.

Philadelphia 1967. Philadelphia Museum of Art. *Master E. S.: Five Hundredth Anniversary Exhibition.* Exh. cat. by Alan Shestack.

Reath, Nancy Andrews. 1927. *The Weaves of Hand-Loom Fabrics: A Classification with Historical Notes.* Philadelphia: The Pennsylvania Museum.

Riefstahl, Elizabeth. 1950. "An Embroidered Tree of Jesse." *The Brooklyn Museum Bulletin* 11 (Summer 1950):5-13.

Ringbom, Sixten. 1965. *Icon to Narrative: The Rise of the Dramatic Close-up in Fifteenth-Century Devotional Painting.* Acta Academiae Aboensis: Humaniora, vol. 31, no. 2. Abo: Abo Akademi.

Robb, David. 1936. "The Iconography of the Annunciation in the Fourteenth and Fifteenth Centuries." *Art Bulletin* 18:480-526.

Rorimer, James J. 1930. "Fourteenth-Century German Altar Cloth." *The Bulletin of the Metropolitan Museum of Art* 25:10-13.

Schapiro, Meyer. 1976. "On the Aesthetic Attitude in Romanesque Art." In *Selected Papers: Romanesque Art* [by Schapiro], pp. 1-27. New York: George Braziller.

Scheyer, Ernst. 1932. *Die Kölner Bortenweberei des Mittelalters.* Augsburg: Benno Filser.

Schiller, Gertrude. 1966-80. *Ikonographie der christlichen Kunst.* 4 vols. Gütersloh: Gerd Mohn.

Schimansky, Dobrila-Donya. 1971. "The Study of the Medieval Ecclesiastical Costumes: A Bibliography." *The Bulletin of the Metropolitan Museum of Art* n.s. 29:313-17.

Schneebalg-Perelman, Sophie.1967. "La Dame à la licorne a été tissée à Bruxelles." *Gazette des Beaux-Arts* ser. 6, 70:253-78.

Schuette, Marie. 1965. "Medieval Tablet Weaving." *Ciba Review* 117:23-29.

Schuette, Marie, and Müller-Christensen, Sigrid. 1964. *The Art of Embroidery.* Translated by Donald King. London: Thames and Hudson.

Schwerin 1983. Staatliches Museum Schwerin. *Kleinkunst, Kunsthandwerk. Mittelalterliche Kunst,* Vol. 2. Coll. cat. by Hans Strutz.

Shepherd, Dorothy G. 1950. "An English Embroidery." *The Bulletin of The Cleveland Museum of Art* 37:66-68.

Shepherd 1953. "A Romanesque Lenten Cloth from Germany." *The Bulletin of the Cleveland Museum of Art* 40:9-10, 15-16.

Shepherd 1954. "A Fifteenth-Century Florentine Embroidery." *The Bulletin of The Cleveland Museum of Art* 41:211-13.

Shepherd 1978. "A Treasure from a Thirteenth-Century Tomb." *The Bulletin of The Cleveland Museum of Art* 65:111-34.

Stechow, Wolfgang. 1968. "A Youthful Work by Stephan Lochner." *The Bulletin of The Cleveland Museum of Art* 55:306-14.

Svec, Evelyn 1952. "A Half-Chasuble with Bohemian Embroidery." *The Bulletin of The Cleveland Museum of Art* 39:189-90.

Toesca, Elena Berti. 1958. *Benozzo Gozzoli: Gli affreschi della Cappella Medicea.* Milan, Amilcare Pizzi Editore.

Uden, Grant. 1968. *A Dictionary of Chivalry.* New York: Thomas Y. Crowell.

Ulrich von Eschenbach, 1888 ed. *Alexander.* Edited by Wendelin Toischer. Bibliothek des literarischen Vereins in Stuttgart, vol. 183. Tübingen: H. Laupp.

Underhill, Gertrude. 1929. "A Textile of the Fourteenth Century." *The Bulletin of The Cleveland Museum of Art* 16:51-52.

Underhill 1930. "A Hispano-Moresque Mantle of the Fifteenth Century." *The Bulletin of The Cleveland Museum of Art* 17:73-74.

Underhill 1931. "Two Fifteenth-Century Brocades." *The Bulletin of The Cleveland Museum of Art* 18:64-66.

Underhill 1939. "Textiles from the H. A. Elsberg Collection." *The Bulletin of The Cleveland Museum of Art* 26:143-46.

Van Marle, Raimond. *See* Marle.

Vocabulary of Technical Terms: Fabrics. 1964. Lyon: Centre International d'Etude des Textiles Anciens.

Von Falke, Otto. *See* Falke.

Von Wilckens, Leonie. *See* Wilckens.

Wagner, Margarete. 1963. *Sakrale Weisstickereien des Mittelalters.* Esslingen: Burgbücherei Wilhelm Schneider

Wardwell, Anne E., 1975. "The Mystical Grapes: A Devotional Tapestry." *The Bulletin of The Cleveland Museum of Art* 62:17-23.

Wardwell 1976/77. "The Stylistic Development of 14th- and 15th-Century Italian Silk Design." *Aachener Kunstblätter* 47:177-226.

Wardwell 1979. "A Rare Florentine Embroidery of the Fourteenth Century." *The Bulletin of The Cleveland Museum of Art* 66:322-33.

Wardwell 1983. "A Fifteenth-Century Silk Curtain from Muslim Spain." *The Bulletin of The Cleveland Museum of Art* 70:58-72.

Weibel, Adèle Coulin. 1952. *Two Thousand Years of Textiles: The Figured Textiles of Europe and the Near East.* New York: Pantheon Books.

Weigert, Roger-Armand. 1962. *French Tapestry.* Translated by Donald and Monique King. London: Faber and Faber.

Wentzel, Hans. 1937. "Almosentasche." In *Reallexikon zur deutschen Kunstgeschichte,* edited by Otto Schmitt, 1:393-401. Stuttgart: J.B. Metzler

Wilckens, Leonie von. 1960. **"Hessische Leinenstickereien des 13. und 14. Jahrhunderts."** *Anzeiger des Germanischen National-Museums 1954 bis 1959.* Pp. 5-20.

Wilckens, Leonie von. 1981. "Eine Stickerei des frühen 14. Jahrhunderts als Bucheinband." In *Documenta Textilia: Festschrif für Sigrid Müller-Christensen,* edited by Mechthild Flury-Lemberg and Karen Stolleis, pp. 275-82. Munich: Deutscher Kunstverlag.

de Winter, Patrick M. 1985. "The Sacral Treasure of the Guelphs." *The Bulletin of The Cleveland Museum of Art* 72 (January-February).

Wixom, William D. 1979. "Eleven Additions to the Medieval Collection." *The Bulletin of The Cleveland Museum of Art* 66: 110-26.

Wyss, Robert L. 1973. "Die Handarbeiten der Maria: eine ikonographische Studie unter Berücksichtigung der Textilien Techniken." In *Artes Minores: Dank an Werner Abegg*, edited by Michael Stettler and Mechthild Lemberg, pp. 113-88. Bern: Stämpfli und Cie.

Zurich [1966/67]. Kunstgewerbemuseum Zürich. *Europäische Textilien*. Coll. cat. by Erika Billeter.

Zurich 1975. Schweizerisches Landesmuseum Zurich. *Textilien: Katalog der Sammlungen des Schweizerischen Landesmuseums Zürich, ausgewählte Stücke*. Coll. cat. by Jenny Schneider.